**OPPOSING
VIEWPOINTS®
SERIES**

P9-BEE-926

Prescription Drug Abuse

Other Books of Related Interest:

Opposing Viewpoints Series
Doping
Health Care
Marijuana

At Issue Series
Alcohol Abuse
Health Care Legislation
Teen Residential Treatment Programs

Current Controversies Series
Medical Ethics
Medicare
Vaccines

"Congress shall make
no law ... abridging
the freedom of speech,
or of the press."

First Amendment to the US Constitution

The basic foundation of our democracy is the First Amendment guarantee of freedom of expression. The Opposing Viewpoints series is dedicated to the concept of this basic freedom and the idea that it is more important to practice it than to enshrine it.

Prescription Drug Abuse

Margaret Haerens and Lynn M. Zott, Book Editors

GREENHAVEN PRESS
A part of Gale, Cengage Learning

GALE
CENGAGE Learning·

Detroit • New York • San Francisco • New Haven, Conn • Waterville, Maine • London

362.299

GALE
CENGAGE Learning®

Elizabeth Des Chenes, *Director, Publishing Solutions*

© 2013 Greenhaven Press, a part of Gale, Cengage Learning.

Gale and Greenhaven Press are registered trademarks used herein under license.

For more information, contact:
Greenhaven Press
27500 Drake Rd.
Farmington Hills, MI 48331-3535
Or you can visit our Internet site at gale.cengage.com

For product information and technology assistance, contact us at

Gale Customer Support, 1-800-877-4253
For permission to use material from this text or product, submit all requests online at www.cengage.com/permissions

Further permissions questions can be emailed to permissionrequest@cengage.com

Articles in Greenhaven Press anthologies are often edited for length to meet page requirements. In addition, original titles of these works are changed to clearly present the main thesis and to explicitly indicate the author's opinion. Every effort is made to ensure that Greenhaven Press accurately reflects the original intent of the authors. Every effort has been made to trace the owners of copyrighted material.

Cover Image copyright © Mahesh Patil/Shutterstock.com.

LIBRARY OF CONGRESS CATALOGING-IN-PUBLICATION DATA

Prescription drug abuse / Margaret Haerens and Lynn M. Zott, book editors.
  pages cm. -- (Opposing viewpoints)
  Includes bibliographical references and index.
  ISBN 978-0-7377-6066-8 (hardcover) -- ISBN 978-0-7377-6067-5 (pbk.)
  1. Medication abuse. 2. Drug abuse. I. Haerens, Margaret, editor of compilation. II. Zott, Lynn M. (Lynn Marie), 1969- editor of compilation.
  RM146.7.P74 2013
  362.29'9--dc23
                                    2012040687

Printed in the United States of America
  2 3 4 5 6   18 17 16 15 14

Contents

Why Consider Opposing Viewpoints?   11

Introduction   14

Chapter 1: Is Prescription Drug Abuse a Major Problem?

Chapter Preface   19

1. There Is a Prescription Painkiller Abuse   22
   Epidemic
   Monifa Thomas

2. It Is Not Clear Whether There Is a Prescription   28
   Painkiller Abuse Epidemic
   Radley Balko

3. Prescription Drug Abuse Contributes to the   44
   Widespread Drugged Driving Problem
   National Institute on Drug Abuse

4. It Is Very Difficult to Determine   52
   the Impact of Prescription Drugs on the
   Drugged Driving Problem
   Angel Streeter

5. "Pharm Parties" Are a Threat to Teen   59
   Health and Safety
   Jeff Mosier

6. "Pharm Parties" Are a Myth   64
   Jack Shafer

7. Mothers' Abuse of Their Children's Medications   69
   Contributes to Drug Supply Shortages
   Katherine Ellison

Periodical and Internet Sources Bibliography   75

Chapter 2: What Causes Prescription Drug Abuse?

Chapter Preface 77

1. Treatments for Chronic Pain Can Lead   79
   to Prescription Drug Abuse
   Liz Szabo

2. Experts Debunk Myths About Prescription   86
   Pain Medication Addiction
   Miranda Hitti

3. Ready Access to Prescription Drugs at Home   95
   Leads Many Teens to Abuse Them
   Sean Clarkin

4. Pharmaceutical Companies Encourage   106
   Physicians to Overprescribe Drugs
   Ellen Ratner

5. Physicians and Pharmaceutical Companies   111
   Should Not Be Blamed for Drug Abuse
   Maia Szalavitz

6. Prescription Drug Abuse Is a By-Product   118
   of Modern American Life
   Lisa Miller

Periodical and Internet Sources Bibliography   131

Chapter 3: How Should Government Policies Address Prescription Drug Abuse?

Chapter Preface 133

1. A Balance of Public Health and Safety Is Best   136
   to Address Prescription Drug Abuse
   R. Gil Kerlikowske

2. Strict Regulation of Prescription Drugs Harms   143
Patients Suffering from Chronic Pain
Elizabeth MacCallum

3. Decriminalizing Drugs Would Reduce   153
Prescription Drug Abuse
David Rosen

4. Decriminalizing Drugs Would Not Prevent   163
Prescription Drug Abuse
William J. Bennett

5. Prescription Drug Ads Should Be   168
Better Regulated
Naomi Freundlich

6. Drug Take-Back Programs Can Limit Access   178
to Prescription Medications
Carnevale Associates

7. An Electronic Prescription Drug Monitoring   186
System Will Guard Against Abuse
Ed Pilkington

Periodical and Internet Sources Bibliography   193

Chapter 4: What Can Be Done to Help Prevent Prescription Drug Abuse?

Chapter Preface   195

1. Doctors Must Improve Patient Screening and   197
Monitoring to Prevent Prescription Drug Abuse
Murtuza Ghadiali and David Pating

2. Physicians Must Warn Patients About the   204
Dangers of Online Pharmacies
Rick Nauert

3. Doctors Who Enable or Facilitate Prescription   210
Drug Overdose Should Be Criminally Prosecuted
Erica Trachtman

4. Parents Can Be Critical in the Prevention   216
   of Teen Prescription Drug Abuse
   Parents. The Anti-Drug

5. Education Is Key in Fighting Prescription   220
   Drug Abuse
   Office of National Drug Control Policy

6. New Technology Can Make Prescription   227
   Drugs More Difficult to Abuse
   Marni Jameson

Periodical and Internet Sources Bibliography   231

For Further Discussion   232

Organizations to Contact   234

Bibliography of Books   240

Index   243

Why Consider Opposing Viewpoints?

> *"The only way in which a human being can make some approach to knowing the whole of a subject is by hearing what can be said about it by persons of every variety of opinion and studying all modes in which it can be looked at by every character of mind. No wise man ever acquired his wisdom in any mode but this."*
>
> *John Stuart Mill*

In our media-intensive culture it is not difficult to find differing opinions. Thousands of newspapers and magazines and dozens of radio and television talk shows resound with differing points of view. The difficulty lies in deciding which opinion to agree with and which "experts" seem the most credible. The more inundated we become with differing opinions and claims, the more essential it is to hone critical reading and thinking skills to evaluate these ideas. Opposing Viewpoints books address this problem directly by presenting stimulating debates that can be used to enhance and teach these skills. The varied opinions contained in each book examine many different aspects of a single issue. While examining these conveniently edited opposing views, readers can develop critical thinking skills such as the ability to compare and contrast authors' credibility, facts, argumentation styles, use of persuasive techniques, and other stylistic tools. In short, the Opposing Viewpoints Series is an ideal way to attain the higher-level thinking and reading skills so essential in a culture of diverse and contradictory opinions.

In addition to providing a tool for critical thinking, Opposing Viewpoints books challenge readers to question their own strongly held opinions and assumptions. Most people form their opinions on the basis of upbringing, peer pressure, and personal, cultural, or professional bias. By reading carefully balanced opposing views, readers must directly confront new ideas as well as the opinions of those with whom they disagree. This is not to argue simplistically that everyone who reads opposing views will—or should—change his or her opinion. Instead, the series enhances readers' understanding of their own views by encouraging confrontation with opposing ideas. Careful examination of others' views can lead to the readers' understanding of the logical inconsistencies in their own opinions, perspective on why they hold an opinion, and the consideration of the possibility that their opinion requires further evaluation.

Evaluating Other Opinions

To ensure that this type of examination occurs, Opposing Viewpoints books present all types of opinions. Prominent spokespeople on different sides of each issue as well as well-known professionals from many disciplines challenge the reader. An additional goal of the series is to provide a forum for other, less known, or even unpopular viewpoints. The opinion of an ordinary person who has had to make the decision to cut off life support from a terminally ill relative, for example, may be just as valuable and provide just as much insight as a medical ethicist's professional opinion. The editors have two additional purposes in including these less known views. One, the editors encourage readers to respect others' opinions—even when not enhanced by professional credibility. It is only by reading or listening to and objectively evaluating others' ideas that one can determine whether they are worthy of consideration. Two, the inclusion of such viewpoints encourages the important critical thinking skill of objectively evaluating an author's credentials and bias. This evaluation will illuminate an author's reasons for taking a particular stance on an issue and will aid in readers' evaluation of the author's ideas.

It is our hope that these books will give readers a deeper understanding of the issues debated and an appreciation of the complexity of even seemingly simple issues when good and honest people disagree. This awareness is particularly important in a democratic society such as ours in which people enter into public debate to determine the common good. Those with whom one disagrees should not be regarded as enemies but rather as people whose views deserve careful examination and may shed light on one's own.

Thomas Jefferson once said that "difference of opinion leads to inquiry, and inquiry to truth." Jefferson, a broadly educated man, argued that "if a nation expects to be ignorant and free . . . it expects what never was and never will be." As individuals and as a nation, it is imperative that we consider the opinions of others and examine them with skill and discernment. The Opposing Viewpoints series is intended to help readers achieve this goal.

David L. Bender and Bruno Leone,
Founders

Introduction

> "Medical science has successfully developed medications that can alleviate suffering, such as opioids for cancer pain and benzodiazepines for anxiety disorders, and allowed more individuals to have access to the medicines they need. However, we all now recognize that these drugs can be just as dangerous and deadly as illicit substances when misused or abused."
>
> —R. Gil Kerlikowske,
> director of the Office of National
> Drug Control Policy, July 18, 2012

On June 25, 2009, the world was shocked when news broke of the death of Michael Jackson at a medical center in Los Angeles. The initial reports stated that the global music superstar had suffered cardiac arrest at his home and had received CPR from his personal physician, Conrad Murray, before being rushed to the hospital. Although the cause of Jackson's cardiac arrest was unknown, it did not take long for friends and associates to speculate that his death stemmed from a longtime and acute dependence on pain-killing prescription drugs. Others pointed to Dr. Murray, suggesting that the physician had enabled and facilitated Jackson's addiction to these life-threatening substances. As Jackson's fans grieved and tributes to his many accomplishments appeared in the media, a firestorm of controversy erupted over the role and responsibility of celebrity doctors and the disturbing trend of prescription drug overdoses among celebrities.

In the days following Jackson's death, Los Angeles police thoroughly investigated the tragedy and quickly realized that the performer's death may have resulted from foul play. Police were seen carrying a number of bags from Jackson's mansion, some of which reportedly contained his large collection of prescription drugs. They also searched Dr. Murray's medical offices in Houston and Las Vegas, confiscating his computer and other important information. Interviews with family and friends confirmed police suspicions about Dr. Murray and Jackson's dependence on prescription medications. Media reports surfaced that Jackson had been able to obtain scores of prescription drugs by using aliases, including the names Omar Arnold and Jack London.

An autopsy performed on June 26, 2009, showed that Jackson died from the combination of drugs in his body. The most significant drugs were propofol, a short-acting anesthetic often used in hospitals to sedate patients for surgical procedures, and lorazepam, a drug used as a sedative or as an antianxiety medication. Also found in his system were midazolam, used as a sedative and muscle relaxant; diazepam, an addictive sleep and antianxiety drug; lidocaine, a local anesthetic; and ephedrine, a stimulant and appetite suppressant. The Los Angeles coroner cited the cause of death as "acute propofol intoxication" in combination with other drugs. Outrage followed when Dr. Murray acknowledged to police that he had administered the powerful anesthetic—which Jackson allegedly called his "milk"—at the singer's request after a grueling day of rehearsals so that Jackson could get some much-needed sleep.

On February 8, 2010, Dr. Murray was charged with involuntary manslaughter in the death of Michael Jackson. The trial started on September 27, 2011, in Los Angeles, and focused on whether Murray had acted with criminal negligence toward his patient and injected him with the propofol that caused his death. On November 7, 2011, Murray was convicted by a jury and sentenced to four years—the maximum penalty for the crime in California.

The testimony from Dr. Murray's trial revealed a seamy side to the relationship between doctor and celebrity patient. It showed that Murray was paid $150,000 a month to act as Jackson's personal physician. Murray stayed with the singer six nights a week and regularly administered propofol and other strong sedatives to the singer at his request so that Jackson could sleep. In fact, the doctor had told police a few days after the singer's death that Jackson had used propofol almost every night. At trial, it also was noted that the doctor had administered the drug without the proper monitoring equipment and had failed to call 911 immediately when Jackson went into cardiac arrest. For many people, Murray's trial revealed an unscrupulous, money-hungry doctor exploiting a high-profile celebrity who was virtually helpless because of his reliance on dangerous and addictive drugs. To others, Murray was so in awe of Jackson and his celebrity that he would do anything the singer demanded to gain his favor and stay in his inner circle. And to some, Murray was viewed as a negligent doctor who failed to monitor his drug-addicted patient's use of prescription drugs and facilitated Jackson's drug overdose.

After the verdict was rendered, Steve Cooley, the Los Angeles County district attorney, expressed his hope that the prosecution of Dr. Murray would discourage other doctors from enabling drug-addicted celebrities for profit or out of ambition. He stated that "in Los Angeles we see many examples of high-profile people losing their lives because of their addiction to prescribed medication. To the extent that someone dies as a result of their playing Dr. Feelgood, they will be held accountable."

With his tragic death, Jackson joined a large group of celebrities who have overdosed from controlled substances; his death cast a light on the ongoing problem of celebrity drug addicts and the doctors who enable their addictions. In recent years, prescription drugs have played a role in the deaths of celebrities such as Heath Ledger, Anna Nicole Smith, and Whitney Houston.

The authors of the viewpoints in *Opposing Viewpoints: Prescription Drug Abuse* explore the consequences of prescription drug addiction in the following chapters: Is Prescription Drug Abuse a Major Problem?, What Causes Prescription Drug Abuse?, How Should Government Policies Address Prescription Drug Abuse?, and What Can Be Done to Help Prevent Prescription Drug Abuse? The information in this volume provides insight into the impact and consequences of the prescription drug abuse problem in the United States, the causes of prescription drug addiction, and proposed and existing government policies that are hotly debated in the ongoing effort to effectively confront the prescription drug abuse problem in this country.

CHAPTER 1

Is Prescription Drug Abuse a Major Problem?

Chapter Preface

In 1995 the US Food and Drug Administration (FDA) approved a new prescription painkiller called OxyContin. By the next year, OxyContin was introduced to the US market. The drug's manufacturer, Purdue Pharma, marketed the drug as a potent painkiller that was virtually addiction proof. By 2001 it was the best-selling non-generic narcotic painkiller in the country. For those with chronic pain, OxyContin turned out to be a godsend for providing long-lasting pain management. Patients who had not been able to find effective pain relief and comfort hailed the drug for its effectiveness, and doctors began to prescribe it for a broad range of medical conditions, from terminal cancer to back pain.

However, the success of OxyContin also had a dark side for patients. It seems that Purdue Pharma was misleading doctors and patients regarding the addictive qualities of the drug. As a time-release form of oxycodone, OxyContin is classified as an opioid and is highly addictive. Opioids are a broad category of drugs derived from natural or synthetic forms of opium or morphine. The best-known opioids are heroin and morphine, both of which are highly addictive. For patients prescribed OxyContin for a valid medical problem, the addiction starts like most others: Patients begin taking the pills as prescribed. After a short time, the patient needs more drugs to get the same benefits. The patient takes more pills, takes them more frequently, or begins crushing the pills to snort or inject to get the drug into his or her system more quickly. Within weeks or months, a patient can be addicted.

With the growing popularity of OxyContin for a number of medical conditions, it wasn't long before law enforcement agencies all over the United States began to report an exploding epidemic of OxyContin addiction in many parts of the country. One of these areas is Florida, which is widely acknowledged to be the epicenter of prescription drug addiction in the United States. Another was the Appalachian area of Kentucky, where the drug became known as "hillbilly heroin." There, doctors frequently treated injured coal miners with OxyContin for years, while a black market for the pills wreaked havoc in communities and families.

Today OxyContin addiction is acknowledged to be a national problem. In 2010 it was estimated that 254 million prescriptions for opioids were filled in the United States. The Centers for Disease Control and Prevention (CDC) pointed out that enough painkillers were prescribed to "medicate every American adult around the clock for a month." It is a problem that affects the rich and the poor, the urban and the rural, the old and the young. As with other addictive drugs, OxyContin addiction can lead to crime, homelessness, social and familial disruption, economic devastation, and even death.

As more and more doctors prescribed OxyContin throughout the late 1990s and 2000s, Purdue Pharma benefited financially. In 2010 sales of OxyContin generated $3.1 billion in revenue. Yet critics charged that the success of the drug was largely built on a misleading advertising campaign that had billed the drug as virtually addiction proof. In 2007 Purdue pleaded guilty to a federal criminal count of misbranding the drug "with intent to defraud and mislead the public." As a consequence, the company paid $635 billion in penalties.

Purdue Pharma also went back to the drawing board and developed a more addiction-proof version of OxyContin. Introduced in 2010, the new version has binding agents, or substances used to hold the pills together, that make it harder to crush the pill—something addicts do to snort or inject the drug. Recent studies have found that many OxyContin addicts have turned to other opioids, like heroin or morphine, to feed their addictions.

The issue of prescription painkiller addiction is explored in the following chapter, which examines the question of whether prescription drug abuse is a major problem. Viewpoints included in the chapter consider the topics of drugged driving and the existence of "pharm" parties among America's youth.

> "Experts say too many people, especially teenagers, mistakenly think that pre- scription drugs are safer and less ad- dictive than street drugs, even when used improperly."

There Is a Prescription Painkiller Abuse Epidemic

Monifa Thomas

Monifa Thomas is a staff reporter for the Chicago Sun-Times. *In the following viewpoint, she points out that prescription drug abuse is the fastest-growing drug problem in the United States, driven by rising rates of abuse for prescription painkillers such as OxyContin, Vicodin, and fentanyl. Although these drugs are ex- tremely effective at relieving pain, Thomas notes, they can be fa- tal when an individual takes them in excess quantities or with alcohol or other drugs. Thomas reports that part of the issue is that people think that because doctors prescribe them, prescrip- tion drugs must be safer and less addictive than street drugs. Health officials, according to Thomas, recommend that more doctors have open and frank conversations with their patients about the dangers of prescription drugs.*

As you read, consider the following questions:

1. What does the Centers for Disease Control and Prevention (CDC) blame for more overdose deaths in 2007 than heroin and cocaine combined, according to the viewpoint?

2. According to the viewpoint, by how much did the rates of treatment admissions for abuse of painkillers and other non-heroin opiates rise nationwide between 1998 and 2008?

3. In what year did Illinois put in place a prescription drug monitoring program, according to the viewpoint?

David and Gail Katz thought their 25-year-old son Daniel had finally turned the corner on his addiction to prescription painkillers after a year and a half of sobriety.

Then, over a two-week period in 2007, Daniel's drug use suddenly "spiraled out of control," his parents said.

On June 15, 2007, Daniel, a well-liked former hockey player, died at his best friend's house after overdosing on Oxy-Contin and cocaine.

"We heard that he had told his girlfriend that he wanted to start again and turn his life around and that night, he overdosed," Gail Katz said.

Some Think Recreational Painkiller User Is Harmless

The Katzes think Daniel started abusing painkillers in college after experimenting with marijuana and alcohol in high school. Though they sought treatment for him several times, Daniel "just couldn't stay sober," Gail Katz said.

The Highland Park [a city in Illinois] couple has since made a full-time job of educating teens and their parents about prescription drug abuse, the fastest-growing drug problem in the United States.

Deaths from unintentional drug overdoses in the United States have increased fivefold over the last two decades, claiming more lives than any other type of accidental injury except car accidents, the federal Centers for Disease Control and Prevention [CDC] reported earlier this year [2011].

Largely driving the trend is rampant misuse of prescription drugs, particularly painkillers such as OxyContin (oxycodone), Vicodin (hydrocodone) and fentanyl.

Abuse of prescription painkillers was responsible for more overdose deaths in 2007 than heroin and cocaine combined, the CDC says.

Rates of treatment admissions for abuse of painkillers and other non-heroin opiates also rose 345 percent nationwide between 1998 and 2008, according to the Substance Abuse and Mental Health Services Administration.

"Five years ago, 70 percent of the people we saw here were heroin addicts. Today, 70 percent of the people we see are prescription drug users," said Jake Epperly, president of New Hope Recovery Center in Lincoln Park.

Misunderstandings About Prescription Drugs

Prescription painkillers, known as opioids, are synthetic versions of opium used to relieve moderate to severe chronic pain.

But in excess quantities, these drugs can suppress a person's ability to breathe. They're especially dangerous when mixed with alcohol or other drugs.

Experts say too many people, especially teenagers, mistakenly think that prescription drugs are safer and less addictive than street drugs, even when used improperly.

"People think, 'It comes from the doctor. Mom took it for a toothache or a broken bone. How bad can it be?'" said Sally

Thoren, executive director of Gateway Foundation, which provides substance-abuse treatment at locations throughout the state.

The surge in prescription drug abuse followed a shift in doctors' prescribing habits that began in the 1990s. Recognizing that they needed to do a better job of managing chronic pain than they had in the past, doctors started writing more prescriptions for pain drugs. Greater availability opened the door for more widespread abuse, said Kathleen Kane-Willis, director of Roosevelt University's Illinois Consortium on Drug Policy.

"In the 80s and early 90s, there was so little pain medicine prescribed," Kane-Willis said. "Now, the pendulum has kind of swung the other way."

There Are Many Contributors to the Spread of Painkiller Abuse

Rather than denying pain medication to people who need it, Kane-Willis said more doctors need to have frank conversations with their patients about the dangers of prescription drug abuse.

Also contributing to the problem are rogue online pharmacies, operating mostly outside the United States, which provide medications to patients who have never seen or talked to a doctor.

Street gangs, too, have become increasingly involved in prescription drug diversion, according to the Chicago field division of the Drug Enforcement Administration [DEA].

Dan, a 30-year-old businessman from Chicago who asked that his full name not be used, has struggled with his addiction to Vicodin for the last eight years. He was first prescribed the drug after a motorcycle accident in 2002.

Before long, Dan, whose family has a history of substance abuse, was going from hospital to hospital, pretending to have

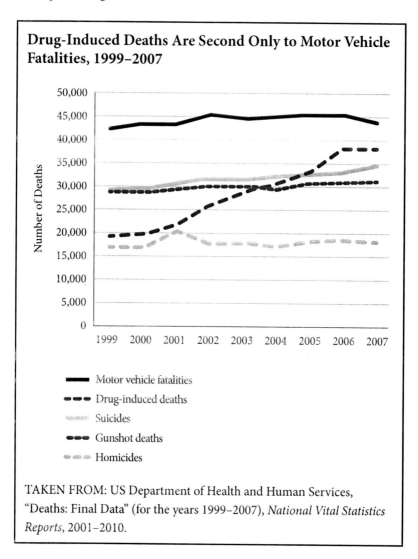

Drug-Induced Deaths Are Second Only to Motor Vehicle Fatalities, 1999–2007

Legend:
- Motor vehicle fatalities
- Drug-induced deaths
- Suicides
- Gunshot deaths
- Homicides

TAKEN FROM: US Department of Health and Human Services, "Deaths: Final Data" (for the years 1999–2007), *National Vital Statistics Reports*, 2001–2010.

shoulder pain, kidney stones and other ailments in order to score more painkillers. At one point, he took as many as 60 to 70 pills a day, often with alcohol.

It Is Too Easy to Obtain Pain Medications

"It's to the point where you can get pain medication as easily as you can get liquor," he said. "All you have to do is say, 'I'm experiencing pain,' and automatically, they're going to give you pain medication to control that. You can use that doctor for probably a month or two before they catch on."

After several failed attempts to get clean on his own, a near-fatal overdose in August led Dan to seek help for his addiction at New Hope Recovery Center. Now, he's cautiously optimistic that the worst is behind him.

"I can't say I'm going to be clean for the rest of my life, but I can promise that when I lay my head down on my pillow tonight, I'll be clean," he said. "I'm taking it one day at a time."

Since 2000, Illinois has had a prescription drug monitoring program that tracks prescriptions filled at retail pharmacies. But the onus is mostly on health care providers to check the database to see whether there's a pattern of doctor-shopping with their patients.

Safe Drug Disposal Is Important

Most people who abuse prescription drugs get them from a friend or family member. To dispose of unused or expired medications safely, don't just throw them in the trash or the toilet, said Janet Engle, head of the department of pharmacy practice at the University of Illinois at Chicago. Instead, remove the medication from its original container, mix it with an undesirable substance like kitty litter or coffee grounds and then throw it out in a nondescript container that can be sealed.

Earlier this year, the DEA and Walgreens launched safe drug disposal programs. Disposemymeds.org is also a resource for finding drug take-back programs in your area.

David Katz said prescription drug abuse will continue to be a widespread problem until the public recognizes that misuse of these drugs can have fatal consequences, as it did for his son.

"Nobody wants to think this could happen to them, but it can," Katz said.

> *"The fact that cocaine-related overdoses have increased at the same rate as opioid-related cuts against the theory that there's been a surge in legitimate pain patients overdosing and dying on painkillers."*

It Is Not Clear Whether There Is a Prescription Painkiller Abuse Epidemic

Radley Balko

Radley Balko is a senior writer and an investigative reporter for the Huffington Post. *In the following viewpoint, he investigates how the United States could have both an epidemic of prescription drug abuse and public health crisis of undertreated pain. Balko finds that US government agencies may be manipulating the statistics on overdose deaths from prescription drugs, attributing a significant number of deaths to opiate overdoses when they could have been caused by something else. He also reveals that after decades of increasingly harsh penalties for doctors for overprescribing pain medications, there are few pain specialists left. Therefore, he asserts, fewer doctors are willing to treat chronic pain; this has caused an explosion of pill mills and unscrupulous doctors willing to endanger patients to profit.*

As you read, consider the following questions:

1. According to an Institute of Medicine report cited in the viewpoint, how many Americans suffer from under-treated pain?

2. According to the viewpoint, how many overdose deaths does the Centers for Disease Control and Prevention (CDC) report there were in the United States in 2008?

3. According to the CDC report cited in the viewpoint, what percentage of prescribers prescribe 80 percent of all prescription painkillers?

"I don't *want* to be doped up all the time," says Mary Maston. "I want to be able to function. I have to be able to function for my kids. But thé pain prevents me from doing so."

In 2008, Maston, 37, was diagnosed with medullary sponge kidney, a congenital disorder that causes her to form large, painful kidney stones. She has since had three lithotripsy surgeries, all of which she says were unsuccessful, and has had to be hospitalized to drain the blood from her kidneys. She has also been diagnosed with stage two chronic kidney disease.

For the first few years after her diagnosis, Maston lived in Tennessee. There, she says, "my doctor was pretty good about writing me a prescription for pain medication when I needed one." But in March 2011, Maston and her family moved to Florida to be closer to her husband's family, and her condition worsened. Florida doctors, she says, were much less willing to prescribe the level of medication she needed. In September, the daily pain from her condition forced her to quit her job. She says she's been to the emergency room seven times in the last eight months, all due to overwhelming pain.

"I always wait until the last possible second, until the pain is so unbearable I am in tears and can't walk," Maston says. "I have a background in Human Resources, so I know [ER visits] drive up everyone's insurance costs. My husband literally carries me to the car to get me to the ER. This is no way to live."

Maston's many ailments are exacerbated by a purely manmade condition. Patients with high cholesterol levels are used to dealing only with their doctor, and not with law enforcement officials, because Lipitor can't get you high. Pain patients, meanwhile, are in the drug war's crosshairs.

The Campaign Against Prescription Painkillers

The most recent campaign against opioid painkillers began last year, when media outlets began reporting an apparent climb in overdose deaths in the state of Florida. As with the scare in the early 2000s, politicians and law enforcement officials scrambled to action, promising new laws and policies to dry up the state's supply of oxycodone. By one estimate, more than twice as many oxycodone pills were prescribed in Florida as the next closest state. Governor Rick Scott signed laws imposing tighter regulations on physicians and pharmacies, testing requirements for patients, limits on overall supply of the drugs, and dedicating more money to law enforcement to fight the alleged epidemic.

Over the last year, the Centers for Disease Control [and Prevention (CDC)] has put out several similar alarming reports using the same term, *epidemic,* claiming a threefold increase in opioid painkiller overdose deaths across the country since 1999. The agency has compared overdose deaths to traffic fatalities (which have been falling steadily for several decades). The CDC believes the significant increase in opioid painkiller prescriptions over the last 10 years is to blame for these deaths, writing in one report, "The unprecedented rise in overdose deaths in the US parallels a 300% increase since 1999 in the sale of these strong painkillers."

But at the same time, studies also consistently show that chronic pain is tragically *under*treated in the U.S. (and around the world). Last June, an Institute of Medicine report called undertreated pain a "public health crisis" that affects 116 million Americans, and costs the economy around a half-trillion dollars per year in medical bills and lost productivity. The same month, three pain-related articles in the *Lancet* focusing on postoperative, cancer-related, and non-cancer-related pain, respectively, found mass undertreatment in all three areas. The journal ran an accompanying editorial pointing to another study from Human Rights Watch showing that the problem is global, and more because of bad policy than because of a supply. In one recent study of 40 countries, 27 didn't consume enough opioid drugs to treat even 1 percent of patients with terminal cancer or HIV/AIDS. "Furthermore," the editorial added, "in 33 of 40 countries, governments had imposed strict restrictions on prescribing morphine, beyond the requirements of UN [United Nations] drug conventions to prevent misuse."

So what's going on? How can we be facing an epidemic of overdose deaths wrought by too many prescriptions for painkillers and, at the same time, be facing a public health crisis of undertreated pain? There are a couple of explanations. The first involves taking a more skeptical look at the numbers the government is touting related to alleged abuse and overdose deaths. The other is to examine how both claims *can* be simultaneously accurate, and why.

The Government Makes Its Case for a Crisis

The CDC (along with the Drug Enforcement Administration (DEA) and the National Institute on Drug Abuse (NIDA)) throws out a number of statistics in making the case for a crisis of painkiller abuse. The first and probably most alarming involves the overdose figures. According to the CDC, painkiller-related overdose deaths have swelled from 4,000 per year in 1999 to nearly 15,000 per year in 2008. The CDC also reports, "The misuse and abuse of prescription painkillers was responsible for more than 475,000 emergency department visits in 2009, a number that nearly doubled in just five years." Most government agencies also classify "abuse" of painkillers as any "non-medical" use, which means any use of a painkiller other than that for which it was prescribed.

But both these figures don't actually mean what they're commonly understood to mean. The emergency room data, for example, is taken from the Drug Abuse Warning Network (DAWN), which compiles the data from the information emergency room patients give to their doctors. Marijuana reform activists have long been critical of how the government manipulates these figures. The government counts any drug a patient mentions having taken, regardless of whether taking the drug is the reason why the patient is in the emergency room. It's *possible* that painkillers sent twice as many people to emergency rooms in 2009 as in 2004, but it's also possible that a good percentage of that increase is simply due to the fact that more people are taking painkillers, and that therefore any given person in an emergency room—for whatever reason—is more likely to mention having recently taken a painkiller. So you twist your ankle in a pickup basketball game. A relative gives you a Percocet they have left over from an old dental surgery to help with the pain. The injury continues to swell, so you visit the emergency room. The government would likely count this as a painkiller-related emergency room incident.

Challenging Overdose Statistics

There are similar questions about the overdose figures. In his 2006 Cato Institute paper "Treating Doctors as Drug Dealers: The DEA's War on Prescription Painkillers," Ron Libby explains how determining overdose deaths is often a guessing game. Back in 2001, Libby notes, the DEA concluded that there were 464 "OxyContin-related" deaths in 2000 and 2001 based on reports from 750 medical examiners across the country. But Libby points out that "OxyContin-related" merely means that the drug was present in an apparent overdose death. If the drug was found in the gastrointestinal tract, it was determined to be an OxyContin-*verified* death. Mere mentions of the drug by family members, or its presence at the death scene, were also enough to count the death as verified. Libby notes that in 40 percent of the deaths in the DEA study, the deceased had also consumed antianxiety drugs like Valium, 30 percent had taken antidepressants, and 15 percent had consumed cocaine.

Libby continues:

> "Indeed, the March 2003 issue of the *Journal of Analytical Toxicology* found that of the 919 deaths related to oxycodone in 23 states over a three-year period, only 12 showed confirmed evidence of the presence of oxycodone alone in the system of the deceased. About 70 percent of the deaths were due to 'multiple drug poisoning' of other oxycodone-containing drugs in combination with Valium-type tranquilizers, alcohol, cocaine, marijuana, and/or other narcotics and antidepressants."

According to the headline-generating CDC report released last November, there were 36,450 overdose deaths overall in 2008. Of those, 74.5 percent specified one or more drugs that were involved in the death. Of those, 73.8 percent involved "one or more" prescription drugs. And of those, 73.8 percent (oddly enough) involved prescription opioids. That likely means that in a high percentage of overdoses attributed to opioids, other prescription drugs were present. In one study of 295 overdose deaths in West Virginia, 80 percent had multiple "contributing" drugs in their system.

Methadone

The drug that has shown the biggest jump in contributing to overdose deaths over the last 10 years is methadone, which is

"The problem is that you're overmedicated. Luckily there are drugs that can help with that." Cartoon by Mike Shapiro. www.CartoonStock.com.

used not just for pain relief, but also as treatment for heroin addicts. Methadone stays in the body longer than commercial opioid painkillers, meaning that without careful attention, it's more likely to lead to an overdose. But it's possible that government policy more than careless doctors has driven any rise in methadone overdoses. Last December, the *Seattle Times* ran an investigative series on the use of methadone in the state. The paper found that state policies for patients who use government-subsidized health care strongly encouraged doctors to prescribe methadone over more expensive brand-name opioids. The result: Methadone made up only 10 percent of opioid prescriptions, but contributed to over half the state's overdose deaths. The drug was prescribed a third as often as OxyContin, but was three times more likely to contribute to an overdose death. If there has been a spike in overdose deaths, it may as much be due to states trying to save money than to doctors who are too loose with the prescription pad.

There's also reason to suspect the raw overdose statistics in and of themselves. Dr. Steven Karch, who has written a widely used textbook on drug abuse and pathology, says because tolerance for opioids can vary so much from person to person, there's no scientific way to definitively say that a death was caused by an opioid overdose. "There are plenty of people walking around with levels of opioids in their bodies that would be declared toxic if they were dead on a slab in a medical examiner's office," Karch says. "Toxicology is the least important part of making a diagnosis."

In other words, many of the deaths classified as overdoses in recent years may in fact have been caused by something else, but were called overdoses simply because the decedent had what appeared to be an abnormal amount of opioids in his system. Karch adds that opium levels can appear more concentrated after death, and can even vary depending on the part of the body from which the sample is taken. It's true that more people than ever are getting prescriptions for opioid painkillers. And as they take them, most people need to titrate up as they build up tolerance. That means a higher percentage of people who die today—of any cause—will have opioids in their systems at the time of death. That doesn't mean they died of an opioid overdose, or even a drug overdose. Many chronic pain patients suffer from a variety of other ailments; it's often those other ailments that cause the pain.

Questionable Diagnoses

"I don't know where they got their numbers," Karch says of the CDC estimates. "There's no peer review of those figures. You follow the footnotes, and it looks like they're getting the information from medical examiners. But it doesn't say how the medical examiners are concluding that these were overdoses—if, say, they're just relying on toxicology results." Asked if that's usually how overdoses are diagnosed, Karch says, "That fits my experience." That the government is using questionable overdose diagnoses in formulating public policy is bad enough, but it's particularly troubling when you consider that some physicians have been charged with manslaughter, even murder, because prosecutors used the same indicators to argue that the painkiller prescriptions caused a patient's overdose death.

The are other reasons to be cautious about the CDC's alarms. . . . Between 1999 and 2006 overdose deaths from cocaine increased at about the same rate as those from prescription opioids. Over that same period, the percentage of youth using cocaine dropped dramatically. The percentage of adults who had used cocaine in the last month stayed about the same. And the number who admitted to using the drug in the last year increased slightly (from 1.7 percent to 2.1 percent, but enough to explain a doubling in overdose deaths), but the number reporting cocaine addiction was down. This suggests that the increases could be due more to changes in methodology, or more awareness and willingness to look and screen for overdose deaths. It could also mean that people who use illicit drugs like cocaine are more likely to use painkillers recreationally because they're more available. But the fact that cocaine-related overdoses have increased at the same rate as opioid-related cuts against the theory that there's been a surge in legitimate pain patients overdosing and dying on painkillers.

Despite the scare stories about teenagers increasingly experimenting with prescription drugs to get high, according to the 2010 National Survey on Drug Use and Health, "nonmedical use" of prescription painkillers in the last year among people aged 12 to 25 has actually dropped since 2002. The same report says overall painkiller "abuse or dependence" is up over the same period, but as explained in part one of this series, "abuse" doesn't necessarily mean using the drug to get high, and "dependence" isn't the same thing as addiction. But the government doesn't make that distinction.

Abuse and Undertreatment

For all the flaws in the data behind the most recent prescription painkiller scare, there's no question that many, many more people are taking them than ever before. It's also likely that plenty of opioid painkillers are making their way to addicts and drug dealers. There are likely more overdose deaths now than in years past, even if there may not be as many as the government claims. Even the most strident advocates for pain patients concede that there are an increasing number of unscrupulous doctors and "pill mills" writing scripts for patients they haven't adequately examined. So how can there be such an abundant supply of painkillers, yet still such a shortage of pain treatment?

The answer lies in some of the government's own data. From a recent CDC "Policy Impact" brief:

> Most prescription painkillers are prescribed by primary care and internal medicine doctors and dentists, not specialists. Roughly 20% of prescribers prescribe 80% of all prescription painkillers.

But the reason so few painkillers are prescribed by pain specialists is likely that after a decade of policies targeting doctors with costly investigations and criminal charges, there simply aren't many conscientious pain specialists left. In his paper for Cato, Ron Libby includes multiple warnings from palliative care specialists that this was exactly what was happening. In 2003, for example, David Brushwood, who is both an attorney and a professor at the University of Florida College of Pharmacy, . . . [said] that physicians once had a cordial relationship with drug cops—that if a doctor suspected a patient was diverting, he would cooperate with the police to turn in the patient. But for the DEA, doctors became high-profile targets, and thanks to asset forfeiture, lucrative targets as well. Since the DEA campaign, Brushwood said, the cops "watch as a small problem becomes a much larger problem . . . [then] they bring the SWAT team in with bulletproof vests and M16s . . . with charges [of] murder and manslaughter."

After a series of high-profile prosecutions of doctors, one pain specialist told the *Wall Street Journal* in 2004, "I will never treat pain patients again." Another told *Time*, "I tend to under-prescribe instead of using stronger drugs that could really help my patients. I can't afford to lose my ability to support my family." The *Village Voice* reported in 2003 that medical schools had begun advising students, "not to choose pain management as a career because the field is too fraught with legal dangers."

Federal prosecutors compared pain specialist William Hurwitz to the Taliban. Other prosecutors and DEA officials have over the years compared doctors to drug kingpins, and likened doctors' offices to crack houses. Some doctors were subjected to SWAT raids on their offices, and had all of their assets seized before trial, making it difficult for them to put on an adequate defense. Prosecutors have called press conferences in which they held up big bags of pills the doctor allegedly prescribed, eliminating all context, and effectively convicting those doctors in the press.

No Safe Harbor

At the same time these high-profile investigations and prosecutions have been going on, the federal government has provided no safe zone for what is and isn't an acceptable way to treat pain with opioids. In fact, they've deliberately blurred the line between acceptable pain management and felonious criminal behavior. In August 2004, for example, the DEA posted a set of pain management guidelines on its website. The guidelines were the product of a three-year collaboration between the agency, several health care organizations, and specialists in the pain management community. They were intended to put at ease doctors and patients who worried that the agency's heavy-handedness was casting a chill over pain treatment. Three months later, the DEA removed the guidelines from its website. The DEA offered no explanation, but the likely reason is that William Hurwitz, the pain specialist the federal government was prosecuting in a high-profile trial at the time, was seeking to use the guidelines in his defense. The guidelines were replaced with an interim statement that emphasized enforcement.

The message was clear. There would be no safe harbor in which pain specialists could operate without worrying about an investigation. There would be no guidelines, and no set policy. What was and wasn't criminal would be decided on an ad hoc basis, worse yet, what was criminal versus what was acceptable medical practice would be determined not by other medical professionals, but by drug cops and federal prosecutors.

A "Chilling Effect"

The DEA's move was so disconcerting that the National Association of Attorneys General sent the agency a letter signed by 30 state attorneys general expressing alarm at the revocation of the guidelines, warning that the new policy would "have a chilling effect on physicians engaged in the legitimate practice of medicine."

But there was and still is a big demand for these drugs. And there's a big supply of them. That has opened a niche for less reputable, less conscientious doctors to open the pill mills and strip mall pain clinics that have sprung up, outfits that dispense hundreds of prescriptions per day. Even the legitimate, careful pain specialists who choose to risk their careers in order to continue to treat pain patients are likely to be overwhelmed with people needing treatment, again making them prime targets for investigation. The successful management of chronic pain requires careful treatment by attentive doctors. The DEA and federal prosecutors have gone a long way to prevent that from happening. Instead, patients get rushed care from inattentive doctors, which is not only less effective, not only more likely to cause drugs to end up in the hands of dealers, it's also dangerous for patients.

Florida's New Law

Lawmakers and law enforcement officials have responded to a crisis created by bad policy with more potent versions of the same bad policy. Even if these new restrictions on how doctors can prescribe pain medication do reduce the amount of the drugs that make it to the streets, addicts and dealers will merely turn to other prescription drugs, or to street drugs. Pain patients don't have that option. (Pain patients could turn to street heroin, but that isn't exactly a desirable outcome.)

Since the new Florida legislation took effect, the pain patient Mary Maston says, "My doctors here very rarely prescribe any type of pain medicine for me, and on the few occasions they do it is for 15 pills. The last time I went to the ER, which was in January, the doctor wrote one for 20 pills, and said that is the maximum the state will allow. When they are gone, they are gone, and I am left to suffer until the pain gets so bad I am forced back to the ER."

Pain patients in Florida and across the country are often asked to take regular drug tests, which they or their insurance are required to pay for, even if they have no history of drug abuse. The few good pain doctors left often err on the side of caution, understandably fearing a possible career-ending investigation. Some require patients to sign a contract promising not to see any other doctors for treatment, even if that doctor concludes that they aren't really in pain. Patients must see their specialist each month to get their prescriptions refilled (assuming they can find one to treat them), and must pay for an office visit each time. There's only a short window to act between the time one prescription runs out and they're legally allowed to obtain a new one. Patients say they're made to feel like addicts. "I'm afraid they have labeled me as a 'drug seeker,'" Maston says.

Secondary Effects of Florida's Law

According to Dr. Albert Ray, president of the Florida Academy of Pain Medicine, the recently enacted Florida law is already having unintended secondary effects, as the major players in pain care show extra caution in deference to the current political climate, which can again leave patients in the lurch. "Baptist Hospital in Miami, one of the best hospitals in town, has a spine care program, with excellent pain doctors directing it," Ray says. "They have decided, however, that they do not want chronic pain patients who need to be maintained on medications." (Ray emphasized that his opinions for this article are his own, and not necessarily those of any organization with which he is affiliated.)

Ray says medication distributors are also limiting the supplies of painkillers they send to pharmacies, and pharmacies have responded to the latest panic with their own new policies. "Some pharmacies, CVS in particular, are now deciding how much medication a patient is allowed to have, not the doctor," Ray says. "These pharmacies won't announce the criteria that they use, but they are sending doctors letters that they will no longer fill their prescriptions for controlled substances. This creates another hurdle for patients."

But it's hard to blame the pharmacies. Even as Ray and pain patients say they're presenting a new hurdle to pain treatment, last week the DEA shut down four Florida pharmacies that the agency says were filling prescriptions they should have recognized were suspicious or fraudulent. More disturbing, the agency also attempted to revoke the license of the drug wholesaler that supplied those pharmacies, a move that threatens to interrupt the supply of medication to 2,500 pharmacies across the South. Any patient who gets controlled medication from those pharmacies could be affected, not just pain patients. (A federal judge has stopped the suspension until a hearing next week [in February 2012].)

Law enforcement agencies have created a system where doctors, pharmacists, manufacturers, and wholesalers have been forcibly deputized to police one another. Given the severity of the penalty—loss of livelihood, even prison time— the overwhelmingly prevailing incentive is to err on the side of control, to halt distribution and report the slightest of suspicions. Some towns and counties in Florida have gone even further, passing yet more restrictions, many of which Ray says, "would bring legitimate pain care to a grinding halt on a day-to-day functional level."

Addressing the Problem

Ray says pill mills and unscrupulous doctors are definitely a problem, but the reaction to them is not only excessive, it overshoots its intended target. "All legitimate doctors want to stop drug diversion and abuse and to close down the pill mills that are violating good medical practice principles for the sake of their greed," Ray says. "But these restrictions are costing the majority of legitimate patients and doctors much frustration, fear, time, energy, and discomfort."

But in that sense, Florida's new law is really no different than the laws that have come before it that have been aimed at controlling drugs with a legitimate medical purpose. The *controlling* abuse side of the ledger takes priority, even when it means restricting access to the drug for the patients who need it.

"We need to view this through the lens that the patient comes first—what they need, and what the best ways are to get it to them," Ray says. "How to get the system to respond in that way remains a frustrating problem."

Mary Maston just wishes the war would be fought elsewhere. "Just because there are people out there that abuse prescription drugs," she says, "that doesn't mean everyone should be punished for it."

> *"Drugged driving is a public health concern because it puts not only the driver at risk but also passengers and others who share the road."*

Prescription Drug Abuse Contributes to the Widespread Drugged Driving Problem

National Institute on Drug Abuse

The National Institute on Drug Abuse (NIDA) is a US government agency tasked with addressing the nation's drug addiction problem. In the following viewpoint, NIDA maintains that the prescription drug epidemic has been a prime contributor to the drugged driving problem, which is caused by drivers under the influence of marijuana or other illicit drugs, over-the-counter medications, and prescription drugs. It is a major problem with teenagers, NIDA maintains, because teens are less experienced drivers and have a higher risk of being involved in serious accidents. Prescription drugs are a particular danger, NIDA concludes, because they act on systems in the brain that impair driving ability.

As you read, consider the following questions:

1. What is a "per se" law, according to NIDA?

"What Is Drugged Driving?," National Institute on Drug Abuse, December 2010.

2. According to the National Highway Traffic Safety Administration (NHTSA) study cited in the viewpoint, what percentage of fatally injured drivers in 2009 had at least one drug in their system?

3. What does the Centers for Disease Control and Prevention identify as the leading cause of death among young people aged sixteen to nineteen, according to the viewpoint?

"Have one [drink] for the road" was once a commonly used phrase in American culture. It has only been within the past 25 years that as a nation, we have begun to recognize the dangers associated with drunk driving. And through a multipronged and concerted effort involving many stakeholders—including educators, media, legislators, law enforcement, and community organizations such as Mothers Against Drunk Driving—the nation has seen a decline in the numbers of people killed or injured as a result of drunk driving. But it is now time that we recognize and address the similar dangers that can occur with drugged driving.

The principal concern regarding drugged driving is that driving under the influence of any drug that acts on the brain could impair one's motor skills, reaction time, and judgment. Drugged driving is a public health concern because it puts not only the driver at risk but also passengers and others who share the road.

However, despite the knowledge about a drug's potentially lethal effects on driving performance and other concerns that have been acknowledged by some public health officials, policy officials, and constituent groups, drugged driving laws have lagged behind alcohol-related driving legislation, in part because of limitations in the current technology for determining drug levels and resulting impairment. For alcohol, detection of its blood [alcohol] concentration (BAC) is relatively simple, and concentrations greater than 0.08 percent have been shown to impair driving performance; thus, 0.08 percent is the legal limit in this country. But for illicit drugs, there is no agreed-upon limit for which impairment has been reliably demonstrated. Furthermore, determining current drug levels can be difficult, since some drugs linger in the body for a period of days or weeks after initial ingestion.

Some states (Arizona, Delaware, Georgia, Indiana, Illinois, Iowa, Michigan, Minnesota, Nevada, North Carolina, Ohio, Pennsylvania, Rhode Island, South Dakota, Utah, Virginia, and Wisconsin) have passed "per se" laws, in which it is illegal to operate a motor vehicle if there is any detectable level of a prohibited drug, or its metabolites, in the driver's blood. Other state laws define "drugged driving" as driving when a drug "renders the driver incapable of driving safely" or "causes the driver to be impaired."

In addition, 44 states and the District of Columbia have implemented [International] Drug Evaluation and Classification Programs, designed to train police officers as drug recognition experts. Officers learn to detect characteristics in a person's behavior and appearance that may be associated with drug intoxication. If the officer suspects drug intoxication, a blood or urine sample is submitted to a laboratory for confirmation.

How Many People Take Drugs and Drive?

According to the National Highway Traffic Safety Administration's (NHTSA) 2007 National Roadside Survey, more than 16 percent of weekend, nighttime drivers tested positive for illegal, prescription, or over-the-counter medications. More than 11 percent tested positive for illicit drugs. Another NHTSA study found that in 2009, among fatally injured drivers, 18 percent tested positive for at least one drug (e.g., illicit, prescription, or over-the-counter), an increase from 13 percent in 2005. Together, these indicators are a sign that continued substance abuse education, prevention, and law enforcement efforts are critical to public health and safety.

According to the 2009 National Survey on Drug Use and Health (NSDUH), an estimated 10.5 million people aged 12 or older reported driving under the influence of illicit drugs during the year prior to being surveyed. This corresponds to 4.2 percent of the population aged 12 or older, similar to the rate in 2008 (4 percent) and not significantly different from the rate in 2002 (4.7 percent). In 2009, the rate was highest among young adults aged 18 to 25 (12.8 percent). In addition, NSDUH reported the following:

- In 2009, an estimated 12 percent of persons aged 12 or older (30.2 million persons) drove under the influence of alcohol at least once in the past year. This percentage has dropped since 2002, when it was 14.2 percent.

- Driving under the influence of an illicit drug or alcohol was associated with age. In 2009, an estimated 6.3 percent of youth aged 16 or 17 drove under the influence. This percentage steadily increased with age to reach a peak of 24.8 percent among young adults aged 21 to 25. Beyond the age of 25, these rates showed a general decline with increasing age.

- Also in 2009, among persons aged 12 or older, males were more likely than females (16.9 percent versus 9.2 percent, respectively) to drive under the influence of an illicit drug or alcohol in the past year.

In recent years, more attention has been given to drugs other than alcohol that have increasingly been recognized as hazards to road traffic safety. Some of this research has been done in other countries or in specific regions within the United States, and the prevalence rates for different drugs used vary accordingly. Overall, marijuana is the most prevalent illegal drug detected in impaired drivers, fatally injured drivers, and motor vehicle crash victims. Other drugs also implicated include benzodiazepines, cocaine, opiates, and amphetamines.

A number of studies have examined illicit drug use in drivers involved in motor vehicle crashes, reckless driving, or fatal accidents. For example—

- One study found that about 34 percent of motor vehicle crash victims admitted to a Maryland trauma center tested positive for "drugs only"; about 16 percent tested positive for "alcohol only." Approximately 9.9 percent (or 1 in 10) tested positive for alcohol and drugs, and within this group, 50 percent were younger than age 18. Although it is interesting that more people in this study tested positive for "drugs only" compared with "alcohol only," it should be noted that this represents one geographic location, so findings cannot be generalized. In fact, the majority of studies among similar populations have found higher prevalence rates of alcohol use compared with drug use.

- Studies conducted in several localities have found that approximately 4 to 14 percent of drivers who sustained injury or died in traffic accidents tested positive for delta-9-tetrahydrocannabinol (THC), the active ingredient in marijuana.

- In a large study of almost 3,400 fatally injured drivers from three Australian states (Victoria, New South Wales, and Western Australia) between 1990 and 1999, drugs other than alcohol were present in 26.7 percent of the cases. These included cannabis (13.5 percent), opioids (4.9 percent), stimulants (4.1 percent), benzodiazepines (4.1 percent), and other psychotropic drugs (2.7 percent). Almost 10 percent of the cases involved both alcohol and other drugs.

Teens and Drugged Driving

According to the Centers for Disease Control and Prevention, vehicle accidents are the leading cause of death among young people aged 16 to 19. It is generally accepted that because teens are the least experienced drivers as a group, they have a higher risk of being involved in an accident compared with more experienced drivers. When this lack of experience is combined with the use of marijuana or other substances that impact cognitive and motor abilities, the results can be tragic.

Results from NIDA's Monitoring the Future survey indicate that in 2007, more than 12 percent of high school seniors admitted to driving under the influence of marijuana in the 2 weeks prior to the survey.

The 2007 Maryland Adolescent Survey indicates that 11.1 percent of the state's licensed adolescent drivers reported driving under the influence of marijuana on three or more occasions, and 10 percent reported driving while using a drug other than marijuana (not including alcohol).

Why Is Drugged Driving Hazardous?

Drugs acting on the brain can alter perception, cognition, attention, balance, coordination, reaction time, and other faculties required for safe driving. The effects of specific drugs of abuse differ depending on their mechanisms of action, the amount consumed, the history of the user, and other factors.

Marijuana

THC affects areas of the brain that control the body's movements, balance, coordination, memory, and judgment, as well as sensations. Because these effects are multifaceted, more research is required to understand marijuana's impact on the ability of drivers to react to complex and unpredictable situations. However, we do know that—

- A meta-analysis of approximately 60 experimental studies—including laboratory, driving simulator, and on-

How Do Prescription Drugs Affect the Brain?

Taken as intended, prescription and OTC [over-the-counter] drugs safely treat specific mental or physical symptoms. But when taken in different quantities or when such symptoms aren't present, they may affect the brain in ways very similar to illicit drugs.

For example, stimulants such as Ritalin increase alertness, attention, and energy the same way cocaine does—by boosting the amount of the neurotransmitter dopamine. Opioid pain relievers like OxyContin attach to the same cell receptors targeted by illegal opioids like heroin. Prescription depressants produce sedating or calming effects in the same manner as the club drugs GHB [gamma hydroxybutyrate] and Rohypnol, by enhancing the actions of the neurotransmitter GABA (gamma-aminobutyric acid). When taken in very high doses, dextromethorphan acts on the same glutamate receptors as PCP [phencyclidine] or ketamine, producing similar out-of-body experiences.

When abused, all of these classes of drugs directly or indirectly cause a pleasurable increase in the amount of dopamine in the brain's reward pathway. Repeatedly seeking to experience that feeling can lead to addiction.

*"Drug Facts: Prescription and Over-the-Counter
Medications," National Institute on Drug Abuse,
May 2012. www.drugabuse.gov.*

road experiments—found that behavioral and cognitive skills related to driving performance were impaired in a dose-dependent fashion with increasing THC blood levels.

- Evidence from both real and simulated driving studies indicates that marijuana can negatively affect a driver's attentiveness, perception of time and speed, and ability to draw on information obtained from past experiences.

- A study of over 3,000 fatally injured drivers in Australia showed that when marijuana was present in the blood of the driver, he or she was much more likely to be at fault for the accident. Additionally, the higher the THC concentration, the more likely the driver was to be culpable.

- Research shows that impairment increases significantly when marijuana use is combined with alcohol. Studies have found that many drivers who test positive for alcohol also test positive for THC, making it clear that drinking and drugged driving are often linked behaviors.

Other Drugs

Prescription drugs: Many medications (e.g., benzodiazepines and opiate analgesics) act on systems in the brain that could impair driving ability. In fact, many prescription drugs come with warnings against the operation of machinery—including motor vehicles—for a specified period of time after use. When prescription drugs are taken without medical supervision (i.e., when abused), impaired driving and other harmful reactions can also result. In short, drugged driving is a dangerous activity that puts us all at risk.

| *"The full impact of drug-impaired driving is hard to gauge."*

It Is Very Difficult to Determine the Impact of Prescription Drugs on the Drugged Driving Problem

Angel Streeter

Angel Streeter is a reporter for the Sun Sentinel, *a South Florida daily newspaper. In the following viewpoint, she maintains that although Florida officials have noticed a sharp increase in the number of drug-impaired driving cases involving prescription drugs, it remains very difficult to ascertain the full impact of drugged driving on public safety. Streeter attributes the problem to several issues—some law enforcement agencies don't adequately distinguish between drug impairment and alcohol impairment; not all law enforcement agencies test for drugs after serious car accidents; and strategies for detecting drug impairment are woefully ineffective. In lieu of standard drug-impairment thresholds, Streeter reports, officers are trained to spot the signs and symptoms associated with drug-related accidents.*

As you read, consider the following questions:

1. According to Streeter, by how much did drug-related automobile crashes increase in Palm Beach County in 2010?

2. What does Streeter identify as the most commonly found drug in deadly car crashes?

3. What government agency does Streeter say is concluding a long-term study to establish crash-risk thresholds for certain drugs?

The scourge of prescription drug abuse is hitting South Florida roads and highways.

Increasingly, drugs such as oxycodone and alprazolam, commonly known as Xanax, are playing larger roles in traffic crashes.

In Palm Beach County, drug-related crashes increased 18 percent last year. There were 64 such cases last year compared to 54 in 2005.

Statewide, drug-related crashes dropped 3 percent last year after climbing nearly 11 percent in 2009. In the last five years, drug-related crashes in Florida increased from 1,176 in 2005 to 1,236 in 2010.

Broward County is "seeing quite a few cases" of drug-impaired driving involving prescription drugs, said Dr. Harold Schueler, chief toxicologist for Broward County's Medical Examiner's Office. But it's unclear if those numbers are increasing.

As all crashes have declined in recent years, so have DUI crashes.

"Prescription-drug abuse certainly makes South Florida's highways and side streets more dangerous any time of the day, not just after happy hour," said Jim Hall, director of the Center for the Study and Prevention of Substance Abuse at Nova Southeastern University.

Police officers, prosecutors and families of victims killed by drivers under the influence of drugs are seeing the results of easy access to prescription medications.

Palm Beach County Assistant State Attorney Ellen Roberts said she increasingly is prosecuting cases in which drug-impaired drivers played a role in deadly crashes.

"Alcohol is still the majority of our prosecutions, but a good percentage of them are other types of drugs," she said. "We're seeing more and more of them."

The antianxiety drug Xanax is the most commonly found drug in the deadly crashes, followed by oxycodone, she said. Perpetrators often are combining them with alcohol. Very few of those drugged-driving cases involve marijuana or cocaine.

That's vastly different from what's happening nationwide. According to the National Highway Traffic Safety Administration, marijuana is the drug most commonly found in drivers, followed by cocaine.

Incidents of crashes involving prescription drugs can be found all over Palm Beach County.

In November, Beruch Zegeye, of Palm Beach Gardens, pleaded guilty to DUI manslaughter in a 2008 crash that killed Paul Krommendyk, 45.

The former Benjamin School student, 19, had a blood alcohol level of 0.072 when he plowed into Krommendyk, who was working his second job as a pizza delivery man, according to police reports. Prosecutors said Zegeye and other Benjamin School students were popping Xanax during a day of partying.

Ena Kane, who lived in west Boca Raton, lost her husband and daughter in a deadly crash in May 2010. Angela Stracar, 26, has been charged with DUI manslaughter and vehicular homicide in the crash.

"My life has been very sad since then," Kane said. "I had a wonderful husband and a wonderful daughter. I had a wonderful life."

Robert and Ena Kane retired to Boca Raton about 20 years ago from New York. In 1995, their only child, Odette Kane, 51, moved here to be near them.

She lived near her parents' Boca Isles South home and visited every night, Ena Kane said.

On May 21, 2010, father and daughter were coming back from picking up dinner, pulling into the Kanes' subdivision, when they were blindsided.

According to investigators, Stracar, of Boca Raton, drove her SUV off the road and smashed through the "Boca Isles South" sign. The SUV went airborne and landed on the Kanes' Cadillac, tearing off the roof.

The Kanes died at the scene.

Blood tests later showed Stracar, whose trial begins in October, had oxycodone, alprazolam, alcohol and THC—the active ingredient in marijuana—in her system.

"They just went out for 15 minutes," said Kane, who lives on the same street as Stracar's family. "Someone like her should not be driving."

Polydrug use, or taking multiple drugs, is common in people who abuse prescription drugs, Hall said.

The typical cocktail is a painkiller, tranquilizer or sedative and a muscle relaxer. That combined use dramatically increases impairment.

"Throw in a beer and you really got trouble," Hall said.

Since oxycodone and Xanax are central nervous system depressants, both cause signs of impairment similar to alcohol, said Schueler, the Broward County toxicologist.

A person taking those drugs may become drowsy and lethargic. Reaction time may be slow.

In fact, the drugs carry warnings on their labels that urge caution when driving after taking the medication, Schueler said.

Boca Raton Officer Fred Laurie is seeing a shift in impaired-driving cases. When he became a police officer 13

Drugged Driving Statistics

- In 2009, 21,978 drivers were killed in motor vehicle crashes nationwide, and 63 percent were tested for the presence of drugs.

- In the same year, 3,952 fatally injured drivers tested positive for drug involvement, representing 18 percent of all fatally injured drivers, or 33 percent of drivers with known drug test results.

- Drug testing rates nationwide increased by 5 percentage points from 2005 to 2009; however, testing rates in the United States varied considerably across states, ranging from 0 to 100 percent.

- Eight states exhibited sizable increases in their testing rates since 2005. Testing rates in all other states remained relatively stable.

- The proportion of fatally injured drivers with known results who tested positive for drugs also varied by state.

- In 2009, narcotics and cannabinoids accounted for almost half of all positive results.

- Positive results involving stimulants decreased by 40 percent since 2005, and the proportion of positive results for narcotics and depressants increased by 36 percent and 39 percent, respectively.

"Drug Testing and Drug-Involved Driving of Fatally Injured Drivers in the United States: 2005–2009," Office of National Drug Control Policy, October 2011.

years ago, most impaired driving involved alcohol. Now, drug impairment is beginning to compete with drunken driving, he said.

"Narcotics are as readily available now as going to the liquor store and getting a case of beer," said Laurie, who is specially trained to detect drug impairment in drivers. "The top three I run into: First are antidepressants (Xanax, Zoloft), second are narcotic analgesics (pain pills), and the third very common one is marijuana."

He points out that having a prescription for those medications doesn't excuse drivers from driving impaired.

The full impact of drug-impaired driving is hard to gauge. Collecting data is difficult because some law enforcement agencies don't distinguish between drug impairment and alcohol impairment, said Ann Howard, spokeswoman for the Florida Department of Highway Safety and Motor Vehicles.

Plus, not all agencies test for drugs in serious crashes.

"It's a hard number to grab," Howard said.

Another challenge is detecting drug impairment. Unlike alcohol, there is no threshold to show a driver is impaired on drugs. In Florida, drivers are considered impaired if they have a blood alcohol level of 0.08.

No similar standard exists for drugs. That's because there are so many drugs that affect the body in so many ways. They also affect people differently and tend to linger in the body long after the effects have worn off.

And not as much research has been conducted on drugs other than alcohol.

The National Highway Traffic Safety Administration is concluding a long-term study that could begin establishing crash-risk thresholds for certain drugs.

Until then, officers such as Laurie are used to identify the signs and symptoms associated with drug impairment.

In prosecuting cases, Roberts said, she focuses on whether or not a defendant had a prescription for the drugs found in his or her blood and how long the person has been taking the medication.

Over time, the longer someone is on a medication, he or she is able to build up a higher tolerance to it. But recreational users still are feeling the effects of the powerful medications.

Still, in the drug-related fatal crashes Roberts has prosecuted, few have had prescriptions.

"*Pharm parties, or pharming, pill or phishing parties, as they're called, can be deadly.*"

"Pharm Parties" Are a Threat to Teen Health and Safety

Jeff Mosier

Jeff Mosier is the education reporter for the Las Vegas Review-Journal. *In the following viewpoint, he reports that government officials in Clark County, Nevada, are increasingly concerned about the growing popularity of "pharm parties," which are parties that center around teenagers taking random prescription drugs. Several deaths have been attributed to pharm parties in the past decade, Mosier explains. Mosier relates the concerns of officials who contend that prescription drugs are easy to get and argues that teenagers often underestimate the risk from taking random pills. Because teenagers usually get pills by taking from their parents, he recommends that parents be more vigilant by securing medications and disposing of unused pills.*

As you read, consider the following questions:

1. According to Clark County Coroner's Office investigator Felicia Borla, as quoted in the viewpoint, how many deaths a year occur at pharm parties in the county?

2. How many cases for possession of prescription drugs on campuses were there in 2011 in Clark County, according to Lt. Ken Young, as quoted in the viewpoint?

3. How many cases of marijuana possession on campus are there every year in Clark County, according to Henderson Police Department spokesman Keith Paul, as quoted by Mosier?

Prescription pills are becoming an increasingly popular drug of choice among teens, in part because of their accessibility.

"Pharm" parties are an emerging trend where an assortment of pills is mixed in a bowl and taken at random by partygoers, police officials said.

A Terrible Risk

These pharm parties, or pharming, pill or phishing parties, as they're called, can be deadly. It happened in 2006 when a girl attended a high school party while the host's parents were out of town. To enter the party, each kid had to donate prescription pills into the bowl.

Everybody was sampling various medications, and a couple of girls became unconscious. Someone panicked and called 911. One girl didn't survive.

Clark County Coroner's Office investigator Felicia Borla, who handled the case, said it's more common than people think, resulting in about four deaths a year.

In another case, a high school boy was having a bad reaction to some pills and went into the bathroom, vomited and passed out on the floor. His friends didn't call for help. Thinking it was funny, they recorded video of him on their cell phones. He never woke up.

Recognizing the Danger

Borla also is a retreat organizer for the [Las Vegas] Metropolitan Police Department's Every 15 Minutes program and has had frank discussions with high school kids about these drugs. Every 15 Minutes is a two-day program involving high school juniors and seniors that encourages them to think about personal safety when alcohol is involved, making mature decisions and recognizing that their actions affect others.

"(Teenagers) state that prescription meds are the easiest things to get a hold of," Borla said. "These juniors and seniors are like pharmacists—they recognize the pills, the numbers on them, the color. They're able to list off meds that I've never heard of like it's nothing.

"They don't view prescriptions really and truly as a drug," she said. "They've told me they're actually fun to mix, (and that) oxycodone and hydrocodone taste good with alcohol."

The Threat of Prescription Drug Abuse

Borla said prescription drug overdoses have increased across the board in recent years, and she expects that to continue.

It doesn't happen just inside the home, either. Lt. Ken Young of the Clark County School District Police Department said there have been about 180 cases for possession of prescription drugs on campuses this school year [2011]. Young said the district averages about 120 cases a year since it began tracking these statistics about five years ago.

Kids may trade or sell pills during school, and police usually don't find out unless a student has an adverse reaction that requires medical attention, Young said.

Unless that happens, or if students or teachers tip off police, kids usually can skate through the school day high.

Assessing the Problem

Young said marijuana continues to be king at school, with about 400 cases each year. Henderson Police Department spokesman Keith Paul said it's difficult to track statistics for prescription drug abuse, and the number of incidents is probably not a good indication of its popularity.

US Trends in Prescription Drug Abuse Among Twelfth Graders

Prescription and over-the-counter (OTC) medications accounted for most of the top drugs abused by 12th graders in the past year. Among 12th graders, past-year nonmedical use of Vicodin decreased from 9.7 percent to 8.0 percent. However, past-year nonmedical use of Oxy-Contin remained unchanged across the three grades and has increased among 10th graders over the past 5 years. Moreover, past-year nonmedical use of Adderall and OTC cough and cold medicines among 12th graders remained high at 6.5 percent and 6.6 percent, respectively.

"Drug Facts: Nationwide Trends,"
National Institute on Drug Abuse, April 2011.
www.drugabuse.gov.

"That doesn't mean they're not occurring," Paul said. "It just means they've not been found out. It usually only happens when there's been an unfortunate overdose."

Detective Tyson Thayer of the Metropolitan Police Department's narcotics division said it's confined mostly to high school students, but he has heard of an increasing number of cases at the middle school level, too. Thayer said students usually deal within their known associates at school as opposed to buying from outside sources, especially adults.

"Some bring whole bottles and some just bring a few extra pills," he said. "It's hard to infiltrate because we're not teenagers," he said.

Addressing Prescription Drug Abuse

Officials agree that parents (and grandparents) can effectively stop the problem from happening if they secure any medications and dispose of unused pills. Parents are the No. 1 source for pills at school. It's easy not to notice one or two pills missing from those orange bottles that definitely aren't childproof.

The Metropolitan Police Department has drop boxes for prescription pills at most of its area commands in the Las Vegas Valley. The Henderson Police Department plans to have such drop boxes available in the next few months. Anyone can drop off unused medications to be destroyed.

The disposal program has been around for about four months, and the department has received about 500 pounds of medication, Thayer added.

> *"No druggie has an incentive to randomly share his parents' OxyContin if there is a chance that all he'll get in return is his pals' over-the-counter allergy meds and Advil."*

"Pharm Parties" Are a Myth

Jack Shafer

Jack Shafer is the media critic for Reuters. In the following viewpoint, he ridicules other media outlets for printing stories about "pharm parties," which he claims have been shown to be a mainstream media myth. Shafer maintains that the stories never quote anyone who actually witnessed such a party, just generic quotes from a drug counselor or cop who claims the parties exist but offers no proof. In addition, he argues that such parties are illogical because drug users are discerning and will not take the chance of taking a random drug when they could just focus on the ones that get them high. Shafer identifies the pharm party myth as the legacy of four decades of "apocryphal drug stories masquerading as news."

As you read, consider the following questions:

1. What were pharm parties known as in the 1960s, according to Shafer?

2. How many times does Shafer say the terms "skittling" or "skittle parties" appear in newspaper stories in the past thirty months?

3. According to Shafer, what TV station finally found a witness to verify the fact that pharm parties exist?

Kids, here's a great idea for a back-to-school party! Run to your bathroom and empty all of your parents' prescription and nonprescription medicines into a bag. Now call all your friends, tell them to do the same, and ask them to meet you at your wackiest friend's house. Next, retrieve the biggest bowl in the house and have everybody dump their pharmacological loot into it. Stir the mass of pills with your hand, call the rest of your friends, and invite each arriving guest to scoop up a handful and swallow as they enter party paradise!

On how many levels is this so stupid it can't have ever happened except as a joke?

Debunking the Myth

If you've read one of my seven previous columns about the "pharm party" myth in which drugs are allegedly shared and consumed in this fashion (June 15, 2006; June 19, 2006; March 25, 2008; March 26, 2008; March 23, 2009; Jan. 21, 2010; and March 17, 2010), you already know that the media keep repeating this tall tale.

To reprise my earlier work, the pharm party myth goes back to the 1960s, when the events were known as "fruit salad parties." The standard pharm party article does not quote a participant, a police officer, or a parent who has actually witnessed the drug event. In most pieces, a drug counselor or a cop is the authoritative source who says the parties are rampant but then offers no proof.

When you think it through, pharm parties are completely illogical. Drug users have always *traded* drugs. But no druggie has an incentive to randomly share his parents' OxyContin if there is a chance that all he'll get in return is his pals' over-the-counter allergy meds and Advil. Drug users are a discerning lot—they read labels and use Internet guides to identify their drugs in the field. As I've written before, they're no more likely to grab a handful of drugs out of a bowl and eat them on the blind chance that they'll get the buzz they want than an attendee at a backyard cookout will drink the first beer he touches at the bottom of the ice chest. Even heavy beer drinkers favor one brand of beer over another.

The Persistent Myth

And yet the myth won't die. In a Sept. 13 feature about addictive pharmaceuticals, *Time* magazine reports:

> This is leading to a rise in the incidence of what's known as skittling, a social phenomenon with deadly consequences. "Kids steal from their parents' medicine chests, go to a party and dump everything into a bowl at the door," says Juan Harris a Hanley [Center] drug counselor. "Anyone who comes in just grabs a handful."

The terms *skittling* or *skittle parties* have also appeared in eight newspaper stories in the past 30 months to describe pharm parties (*Grand Rapids Press*, April 4, 2008; the *Oklahoman*, July 27, 2008; *Wyoming Tribune-Eagle*, Dec. 10, 2008; the Bloomington, Ill., *Pantagraph*, May 23, 2009; the Rock Hill, S.C., *Herald*, July 19, 2009 . . . ; the North Carolina *Fort Mill Times*, Dec. 11, 2009, . . . ; Manchester, New Hampshire's WMUR-TV, Feb. 22, 2010; the Westchester County, N.Y., *Journal News*, March 11, 2010, . . . ; and the Westchester County *Journal News* again, April 9, 2010).

Meanwhile, in the past six months, the term *pharm parties* has appeared in the *Virginian-Pilot*, Feb. 7, 2010; on CNN's *Issues with Jane Velez-Mitchell*, March 1, 2010, in which Marie Osmond talks about them in a *Larry King Live* tape; North Carolina's *Asheville Citizen-Times*, March 17, 2010; the *Cincin-*

nati Enquirer, April 12, 2010; the *Albany Times Union,* April 15, 2010, . . . ; *Tulsa World,* April 16, 2010; Florida's *Stuart News,* April, 18, 2010; Oklahoma's *Woodward News,* April 30, 2010; South Dakota's *Argus Leader,* May 23, 2010, . . . ; Harrisburg, Pa.'s WHP-TV, June 18, 2010; North Carolina's *Richmond County Daily Journal,* June 22, 2010; Connecticut's *News-Times,* Aug. 16, 2010; and the *Washington Post,* Aug. 24, 2010.

Do Pharm Parties Exist?

In none of these stories or mentions—including this week's *Time* piece—is a specific pharm party mentioned or a police report cited. They're all generic mentions, often coming from the lips of drug counselors or cops talking about the "problem." But sometimes the police actually talk sense. When the *Fort Mill Times* asks the head of York County's drug enforcement unit about skittle parties and pharm parties, he says plenty of people are doing pills, but no police records exist to document the pharm parties people are talking about.

"We haven't seen it ourselves," the drug cop tells the newspaper. "We hear about them when we arrest somebody."

A Witness

But evidence that you should never say never comes from WHSV-TV in Harrisonburg, Va. In its June 21, 2010, report, the station quotes and names a 17-year-old who says he attended a pharm party! At last, a first-person take, direct from the scene of the bacchanal!

"While I was hanging out with them, they asked me if I wanted to go to a pharm party," the young man tells WHSV. "I never knew what it was, so I said sure." The young man told the station that he was shocked to see other kids taking random meds from a bowl and washing them down with alcohol. He says he did not join in.

We can believe that the young man is lying about the pharm party. Or that he's exaggerating. Or that he is confusing what he saw with what he has heard talked about. Or we can believe he's telling the absolute truth and that after four decades of apocryphal drug stories masquerading as news, life is now imitating fiction, and kids are finally munching random drugs.

Me? I'll believe it when I hear it from the drug-eaters themselves.

> *"The danger comes when people with-*
> *out [attention-deficit/hyperactivity dis-*
> *order] take the meds to boost their pro-*
> *ductivity, a trap experts say has of late*
> *become especially tempting for young*
> *mothers."*

Mothers' Abuse of Their Children's Medications Contributes to Drug Supply Shortages

Katherine Ellison

Katherine Ellison is a Pulitzer Prize–winning former foreign cor-
respondent and author, most recently, of Buzz: A Year of Paying
Attention. *In the following viewpoint, she investigates a growing*
trend: young mothers abusing their children's attention-deficit/
hyperactivity disorder (ADHD) medicine to improve their own
energy and productivity levels. Ellison reports that the increasing
popularity of ADHD drugs like Adderall and Ritalin have re-
sulted in not only college and high school kids abusing the medi-
cations but their mothers abusing it as well. Women must be
aware of the signs of addiction and its consequences, Ellison
notes.

As you read, consider the following questions:

1. According to Ellison, from 2002 to 2010, how much has Adderall use surged with women over the age of twenty-six?

2. How many ADHD drugs were sold in 2010, according to the author?

3. According to the National Institute on Drug Abuse data cited in the viewpoint, from 2008 to 2010, how much did abuse of stimulants increase among high school seniors?

All over the country in recent weeks, mothers of children with attention-deficit/hyperactivity disorder [ADHD] have been scrambling to fill prescriptions for their kids' stimulant medications due to suddenly scarce supplies.

Drug firms blame the shortage on quotas of the psychoactive ingredients, set by the U.S. Drug Enforcement Administration [DEA] to control abuse. Some DEA officials counter that the drug firms have chosen to use their limited allotments to make more of the pricey, brand-name drugs, causing a dearth of the cheaper generics.

Manufacturing issues aside, however, the National Institute on Drug Abuse suggests there may be another reason for the stimulant shortages: a dramatic increase in their use—and abuse—by women of childbearing age.

The Rise of ADHD Drugs

Over the last decade, the number of prescriptions written each year for generic and brand-name forms of Adderall, an amphetamine mix that has recently become the most popular ADHD remedy, has surged among women over 26, rising from a total of roughly 800,000 in 2002 to some 5.4 million in 2010. A particularly startling increase has been for women aged 26 to 39, for whom prescriptions soared by 750 percent.

Though part of this rise can be accounted for by an increase in population, officials at the National Institute on Drug Abuse are concerned that it is widening the pipeline for diversion and abuse.

Many doctors recommend stimulants for children and adults who have symptoms of ADHD, including difficulty sustaining attention and maintaining self-control. Experts in the field say they help strengthen the parts of the brain involved in these functions by improving the utilization of dopamine, a key neurotransmitter.

Yet amphetamines and other stimulants can also be abused, especially when crushed and snorted, providing a "rush" that has been compared to that of cocaine. The American Society of Health-System Pharmacists warns that even when taken as prescribed, the medications can be habit forming, and also have possibly serious side effects, including seizures, paranoia, aggressive behavior and tics. In people with preexisting heart problems, there is an added danger of cardiac arrest.

The upside of the medications—their ability to help those with attention-deficit disorders to focus—has nonetheless led to a continuing increase in their use, and in drug company revenue. In 2010, manufacturers sold $7.42 billion worth of the drugs, up from $4.05 billion just two years earlier.

Many of these new prescriptions are warranted. When ADHD symptoms are severe, the disorder can be debilitating for children and adults. As stigma surrounding it has abated, it's not surprising that there has been an increase in adults, in particular, seeking treatment.

"Mother's Little Helper"

The danger comes when people without ADHD take the meds to boost their productivity, a trap experts say has of late become especially tempting for young mothers. Remember that *Desperate Housewives* episode in which actress Felicity Huff-

What Are Stimulants?

As the name suggests, stimulants increase alertness, attention, and energy, as well as elevate blood pressure, heart rate, and respiration. Stimulants historically were used to treat asthma and other respiratory problems, obesity, neurological disorders, and a variety of other ailments. But as their potential for abuse and addiction became apparent, the medical use of stimulants began to wane. Now, stimulants are prescribed to treat only a few health conditions, including ADHD [attention-deficit/hyperactivity disorder], narcolepsy, and occasionally depression—in those who have not responded to other treatments.

"Prescription Drugs: Abuse and Addiction,"
National Institute on Drug Abuse, 2011. www.drugabuse.gov.

man tries her kids' Ritalin and finds it's the perfect "mother's little helper" as she races to finish making costumes for the school performance of "Little Red Riding Hood"?

"Much as kids are stressed by having to go through school and all their outside activities, their moms are right there with them," says Stephen Odom, a Newport Beach addiction specialist. "She's more tired than anyone, and coffee just doesn't do it."

Like the Huffman character, many women start out by sampling their children's meds—a felony, by the way. Then they get prescriptions of their own, sometimes by faking ADHD symptoms, or find the pills by more underhanded means.

This was the case for Sunny Morrisette, a 28-year-old woman in Logan, Utah, arrested last month for trading cigarettes to neighborhood schoolchildren in return for their

ADHD drugs. Ms. Morrisette allegedly told police that she was under a lot of stress and had heard "good things about Adderall and wanted to try it." She was charged with several felony drug offenses and with contributing to the delinquency of a minor.

"There's a lot of denial around these drugs, and the danger is easy to minimize because that prescription label can make you feel what you're doing is safe," warns Brad Lamm, the president of a New York intervention agency.

ADHD in Colleges and High Schools

The greatest rates of abuse continue to be found on college campuses, where students use the meds to study—and party— harder. Dee Owens, director of the Alcohol-Drug Information Center at Indiana University, says Adderall abuse has become "epidemic among young ladies" who are trying to keep their grades up and their weight down, and to drink more beer without falling asleep.

More worrisome, and in what the National Institute on Drug Abuse calls a "cause for alarm," abuse of prescription stimulants is also becoming more prevalent in high school. An institute survey of 45,000 students found abuse of stimulants had increased among high school seniors, from 6.6 percent to 8.2 percent in just the last two years.

Full disclosure: I've been diagnosed with ADHD myself—by three different experts—and I've recently started to take Adderall on occasion, with some mixed feelings. The good part is a boost in my energy and mood, which makes sense, considering that back in the 1930s many doctors prescribed amphetamines to treat depression. Yet I worry about becoming dependent.

Signs of Addiction

That's one reason why, knowing just how many of my busy fellow mothers are relying on amphetamines, I've asked experts for their advice about how to watch for signs of addiction.

Here's what they tell me: Make sure you take pills only under a doctor's supervision. Don't fall in the trap of boosting your dose. And get help right away if you catch yourself lying about your use or getting prescriptions from more than one doctor.

"Just like with any drug, if you can't stop, despite adverse consequences, you have an issue," says Dee Owens, who has worked in addiction prevention for more than 20 years. "I've talked to hundreds—no—thousands of people, and not a single person ever meant to become an addict. They just wake up one day—and there they are."

Periodical and Internet Sources Bibliography

The following articles have been selected to supplement the diverse views presented in this chapter.

Manny Alvarez	"Teen Drug Abuse Becoming an Epidemic, Must Be Addressed," FoxNews.com, May 2, 2012.
Nicole Brochu	"'Oxy Express' Gives Birth to New Problem: Drug-Addicted Babies," SunSentinel.com, July 28, 2012.
Deanna Goeman	"Be Aware of Prescription Drugs' Effects Before Driving," *Plain Talk* (Vermillion, South Dakota), February 24, 2012.
Jenna Johnson	"College Administrators Worry That Use of Prescription Stimulants Is Increasing," *Washington Post*, November 27, 2011.
Sheryl Marsh	"Candy Not at Skittles Parties," *Decatur Daily* (Alabama), April 3, 2011.
Justin T. Palm	"Drug Abuse—A Global Epidemic. Part 2: Scope of the Problem," *The Real Truth*, July 16, 2012.
Alice Park	"Teens and Drugs: Rite of Passage or Recipe for Addiction?," *Time*, June 29, 2011.
Jessica Samakow	"Prescription Drug Abuse: Report Calls Parent Pill Popping an 'Epidemic,'" *Huffington Post*, May 14, 2012.
Marianne Skolek	"It's Not All About 'Abuse'—Let's Tell It Like It Is—It's 'Addiction' and Pharma and the FDA Is Responsible for It," Salem-News.com, July 29, 2012.
Lindsey Tanner	"Vets Prone to Drug Addiction Get Risky Pain-killers," Associated Press, March 6, 2012.

OPPOSING
VIEWPOINTS®
SERIES

CHAPTER 2

What Causes Prescription Drug Abuse?

Chapter Preface

Chronic pain is an epidemic in the United States. Health authorities estimate that it affects more than seventy million Americans, making it more common than heart disease, cancer, and diabetes combined. An estimated 20 percent of children suffer from it. It is also estimated that chronic pain costs the US economy more than $100 billion each year. Yet despite the costs and the gravity of the problem, many people believe that doctors and researchers are not taking the issue of chronic pain seriously enough, and that they fail to provide effective pain management for patients suffering with daily, excruciating pain.

In general, chronic pain is defined as pain lasting long past the onset or injury, or extends past the accepted healing period. Pain lasting for a short time—from a month to three months—is usually known as acute pain. Once a person experiences a consistent level of pain for more than six months, however, it is considered chronic pain and an illness in its own right.

There are two general types of chronic pain: nociceptive pain is caused by the activation of nociceptors, which are pain receptors in the skin, cornea, and a variety of organs that send nerve signals to the brain and spinal cord; and neuropathic pain, which originates in the peripheral nervous system, brain, or spinal cord. The level of pain can be mild or excruciating; episodic or continuous; merely bothersome or utterly incapacitating. Chronic pain can last for weeks or months—even years.

The start of chronic pain may stem from an injury or infection, or there may be an ongoing cause of pain. The most common sources of chronic pain are headaches, back and joint problems, cancer, tendonitis, sinus issues, and carpal tunnel syndrome. It has been observed that generalized muscle or nerve pain can also evolve into a chronic condition. Growing numbers of people report chronic pain despite no evidence of any past injury or trauma.

In recent years, many public health officials have concluded that the current health system is not effectively addressing the problem of chronic pain. According to a 2009 report by the Mayday Fund, "patients with persistent pain often find themselves in an endless cycle, seeing multiple health care providers, including many specialists in areas other than pain, who are not prepared to respond effectively. They often endure repeated tests and inadequate or unproven treatments. This may include unnecessary surgeries, injections or procedures that have no long-term impact on comfort and function. Patients with chronic pain have more hospital admissions, longer hospital stays, and unnecessary trips to the emergency department. Such inefficient and even wasteful treatment for pain is contributing to the rapid rise in health care costs in the United States."

The use of prescription painkillers for chronic pain has generated debate in the public health community. Although drugs have been proven very effective for pain management for many types of chronic pain, there is also a danger of abuse. Prescription painkillers like Percocet and OxyContin are highly addictive drugs. Many health professionals prefer other pain management strategies, including acupuncture, biofeedback, electrical stimulation, and exercise.

The link between chronic pain and prescription painkiller addiction is one of the topics discussed in the following chapter, which explores the causes of prescription drug abuse. Other viewpoints in the chapter examine the role of the Internet in obtaining cheap prescription drugs; the culpability of pharmaceutical companies, physicians, and pharmacists in overprescribing prescription drugs; and the responsibility of parents in limiting the availability of drugs in the home.

| "Addiction to prescription painkillers— which kill thousands of Americans a year—has become a largely unrecognized epidemic, experts say."

Treatments for Chronic Pain Can Lead to Prescription Drug Abuse

Liz Szabo

Liz Szabo is a reporter for USA Today. *In the following viewpoint, she investigates the troubling trend of prescription painkiller abuse, a problem largely caused when a patient with chronic pain becomes addicted to his or her prescription pain medication. She reports that prescription painkillers have surpassed heroin and cocaine as the leading cause of fatal overdoses. Szabo states that patients fall into prescription painkiller abuse because such drugs are easy to get from doctors, and patients become dependent on the psychological benefits after the physical pain has subsided. These addictions are difficult to detect and are often missed by doctors, Szabo explains. She suggests that doctors must be more vigilant and that a nationwide electronic medical records system would help in monitoring a patient's drug prescriptions.*

As you read, consider the following questions:

1. How many deaths does the Centers for Disease Control and Prevention (CDC) estimate were caused by opioid painkiller overdose, according to data cited in the viewpoint?

2. According to Laxmaiah Manchikanti, as quoted in the viewpoint, how many Americans go to the emergency room after overdosing on opioid painkillers every year?

3. How many states does Laxmaiah Manchikanti say have electronic databases to track narcotics prescriptions, according to the viewpoint?

Debra Jones didn't begin taking painkillers to get high.

Jones, 50, was trying to relieve chronic pain caused by rheumatoid arthritis.

Yet after taking the painkiller Percocet safely for 10 years, the stay-at-home mother of three became addicted after a friend suggested that crushing her pills could bring faster relief. It worked. The rush of medication also gave her more energy. Over time, she began to rely on that energy boost to get through the day. She began taking six or seven pills a day instead of the three to four a day as prescribed.

"I wasn't trying to abuse it," says Jones, from Holly Springs, N.C., who has since recovered from her battle with addiction. "But after 10 years, I couldn't help what it did to my body or my brain. It was hard to work without it."

An Epidemic

Addiction to prescription painkillers—which kill thousands of Americans a year—has become a largely unrecognized epidemic, experts say. In fact, prescription drugs cause most of the more than 26,000 fatal overdoses each year, says Leonard Paulozzi of the Centers for Disease Control and Prevention [CDC].

The number of overdose deaths from opioid painkillers—opium-like drugs that include morphine and codeine—more than tripled from 1999 to 2006, to 13,800 deaths that year, according to CDC statistics released Wednesday [in August 2010].

In the past, most overdoses were due to illegal narcotics, such as heroin, with most deaths in big cities. Prescription painkillers have now surpassed heroin and cocaine, however, as the leading cause of fatal overdoses, Paulozzi says. And the rate of fatal overdoses is now about as high in rural areas—7.8 deaths per 100,000 people—as in cities, where the rate is 7.9 deaths per 100,000 people, according to a paper he published last year in *Pharmacoepidemiology and Drug Safety*.

"The biggest and fastest-growing part of America's drug problem is prescription drug abuse," says Robert DuPont, a former White House drug czar and a former director of the National Institute on Drug Abuse. "The statistics are unmistakable."

About 120,000 Americans a year go to the emergency room after overdosing on opioid painkillers, says Laxmaiah Manchikanti, chief executive officer and board chairman for the American Society of Interventional Pain Physicians.

More Sales, More Addicts

Experts say it's easy to see why so many Americans are abusing painkillers.

There are lots of the drugs around, and they're relatively easy to get, says David Zvara, chair of anesthesiology at University of North Carolina Hospitals.

As Americans age and carry extra pounds, more are asking for pain relief to cope with joint problems, back pain and other ailments, Zvara says. He says he has seen a huge increase in the number of patients seeking care for chronic pain.

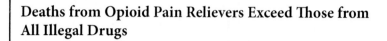

Deaths from Opioid Pain Relievers Exceed Those from All Illegal Drugs

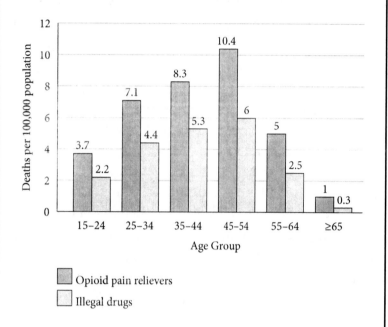

TAKEN FROM: Centers for Disease Control and Prevention, "Vital Signs: Overdoses of Prescription Opioid Pain Relievers—United States, 1999–2008," *Morbidity and Mortality Weekly Report*, vol. 60, no. 43, p. 1489, 2011.

Paulozzi notes that the rise in fatal overdoses almost exactly parallels a corresponding rise in prescription painkiller sales. In surveys, about 5% of Americans say they have used a prescription narcotic in the past month.

Doctors today are also more apt to prescribe pain pills in an effort to relieve real suffering, says James Garbutt, a UNC [University of North Carolina] addiction specialist.

Of course, many people take painkillers legally and carefully follow their doctors' prescriptions. The medical profession has paid more attention to adequate pain relief for terminal cancer patients, for example, who aren't in danger of addiction, Zvara says.

But some people are genetically susceptible to addiction, especially if they have a family history of it, says Nora Volkow, director of the National Institute on Drug Abuse.

People are also at higher risk of addiction if they are depressed or under stress, because many people find that painkillers provide a sense of well-being or euphoria, Volkow says. Some begin to rely on these psychological benefits long after their physical pain has subsided.

Doctor Shopping

Many abusers go from doctor to doctor for new prescriptions. Others, when turned down by doctors, buy painkillers on the street or through illegal Internet sites, Manchikanti says.

It's also easy for addicts to overdose. Although these drugs are safe when taken as directed, taking high doses can make people stop breathing.

"At the high doses used by drug abusers, the margin of safety is small," Paulozzi says. "Combining such drugs on your own or using them with alcohol increase the risk."

Getting Help

Because persistent pain and painkillers can carry so many risks, people with pain that lasts more than three months should consult a pain management specialist, says Christopher Gharibo, medical director of pain medicine at NYU [Langone Medical Center's] Hospital for Joint Diseases in New York.

To treat long-term pain, doctors may try a combination approach, using anti-inflammatory drugs, anti-convulsants and muscle relaxants, Gharibo says. For lower back pain, for example, doctors may use anesthetic patches and "trigger-point injections" into specific muscles, he says.

To prevent patients from abusing or selling their painkillers, doctors may do unannounced urine tests or count a patient's remaining pills, Manchikanti says. He says patients need to accept that they may never be completely free of pain.

Instead, he says his goal is to help patients to "be active and functional without escalating their dosage."

Krista Smith, 39, takes the narcotic Vicodin to relieve the lingering pain caused by a car accident 23 years ago, when she was burned on over 80% of her body. But Smith uses them sparingly—making a bottle of 50 pills last four months—to avoid becoming addicted.

"I deal with pain every day," says Smith, a mother of two from Timberville, Va. "I've been through so much pain that I guess I can tolerate a lot."

Many doctors say that preventing abuse requires a national effort.

Although 39 states have electronic databases to track narcotics prescriptions, none share that information fully with other states, Manchikanti says. So patients who get narcotics in one state may be able to cross the state line to get more.

A nationwide system of electronic medical records also would help, Zvara says, because doctors in different hospitals and clinics would easily be able to measure how many narcotics doses a patient has had.

Easy to Underestimate

Experts say there are many reasons why the public—and even doctors—don't realize the seriousness of the problem. Unlike crack, prescription painkillers generally aren't associated with increased street crime or violence, Zvara says.

And Volkow notes that many people underestimate how lethal painkillers can be, assuming that anything prescribed by a doctor must be safe.

Experts say Jones was lucky to get help before it was too late.

Jones says she tried and failed to quit the drug on her own. Although she never spent more than about $50 at a time buying extra pills from "acquaintances of acquaintances," Jones says she realized she was becoming dependent on them.

She eventually kicked the habit through a UNC program and has been clean for two years. She now takes a methadone-like drug for pain.

"I can't tell you how good it feels to be off of it," Jones says. "I never dreamed it could be so addictive or dangerous. It's something you don't know about until you live it."

"Many people mistakenly use the term 'addiction' to refer to physical dependence. That includes doctors."

Experts Debunk Myths About Prescription Pain Medication Addiction

Miranda Hitti

Mirandi Hitti is senior medical writer for WebMD. In the following viewpoint, she lists seven myths about prescription painkiller abuse and addresses the major problem that physical dependence on painkillers is often mistaken for addiction. Hitti points out that addiction experts state that physical dependence can include symptoms of addiction but that the two are different conditions. She also reports that the general public believes several other myths about addiction, including that everyone will eventually become addicted to painkillers if they take them long enough; it is okay to adjust the dosage without a doctor's consent; it is better to take the pain than to risk addiction; pain relief is the only thing that matters; and a patient's doctor will effectively monitor a patient's drug intake and prevent addiction.

As you read, consider the following questions:

1. What is Scott Fishman's definition of addiction, as cited in the viewpoint?

2. According to government statistics cited in the viewpoint, how many Americans age twelve and older abused or were addicted to pain relievers in 2007?

3. According to a 2007 survey cited in the viewpoint, what percentage of Americans who reported taking pain relievers for "nonmedical" uses in the past month said they'd gotten pain pills for free?

Prescription pain medicine addiction grabs headlines when it sends celebrities spinning out of control. It also plagues many people out of the spotlight who grapple with painkiller addiction behind closed doors.

But although widespread, addiction to prescription painkillers is also widely misunderstood—and those misunderstandings can be dangerous and frightening for patients dealing with pain.

Where is the line between appropriate use and addiction to prescription pain medicines? And how can patients stay on the right side of that line, without suffering needlessly? For answers, WebMD spoke with two pain medicine doctors, an expert from the National Institute on Drug Abuse, and a psychiatrist who treats addictions.

Here are seven myths they identified about addiction to prescription pain medication.

1. Myth: If I need higher doses or have withdrawal symptoms when I quit, I'm addicted.

Reality: That might sound like addiction to you, but it's not how doctors and addiction specialists define addiction.

"Everybody can become tolerant and dependent to a medication, and that does not mean that they are addicted," says

Christopher Gharibo, MD, director of pain medicine at the NYU Langone Medical Center and NYU Hospital for Joint Diseases.

Tolerance and dependence don't just happen with prescription pain drugs, notes Scott Fishman, MD, professor of anesthesiology and chief of the division of pain medicine at the University of California, Davis School of Medicine.

"They occur in drugs that aren't addictive at all, and they occur in drugs that are addictive. So it's independent of addiction," says Fishman, who is the president and chairman of the American Pain Foundation and a past president of the American Academy of Pain Medicine.

Many people mistakenly use the term "addiction" to refer to physical dependence. That includes doctors. "Probably not a week goes by that I don't hear from a doctor who wants me to see their patient because they think they're addicted, but really they're just physically dependent," Fishman says.

Fishman defines addiction as a "chronic disease … that's typically defined by causing the compulsive use of a drug that produces harm or dysfunction, and the continued use despite that dysfunction."

For instance, someone who's addicted might have symptoms such as "having drugs interfere with your ability to function in your role [or] spending most of your time trying to procure a drug and take the drug," says Susan Weiss, PhD, chief of the science policy branch at the National Institute on Drug Abuse.

"Physical dependence, which can include tolerance and withdrawal, is different," says Weiss. "It's a part of addiction but it can happen without someone being addicted."

She adds that if people have withdrawal symptoms when they stop taking their painkiller, "it means that they need to be under a doctor's care to stop taking the drugs, but not necessarily that they're addicted."

2. Myth: Everyone gets addicted to pain drugs if they take them long enough.

Reality: "The vast majority of people, when prescribed these medications, use them correctly without developing addiction," says Marvin Seppala, MD, chief medical officer at the Hazelden Foundation, an addiction treatment center in Center City, Minn.

Fishman agrees. "In a program where these prescription drugs are used with responsible management, the signs of addiction or abuse would become evident over time and therefore would be acted on," says Fishman.

Some warning signs, according to Seppala, could include raising your dose without consulting your doctor, or going to several doctors to get prescriptions without telling them about the prescriptions you already have. And as Weiss points out, being addicted means that your drug use is causing problems in your life but you keep doing it anyway.

But trying to diagnose early signs of addiction in yourself or a loved one can be tricky.

"Unless you really find out what's going on, you'd be surprised by the individual facts behind any patient's behavior. And again, at the end of the day, we're here to treat suffering," says Fishman.

Likewise, Weiss says it can be "very, very hard" to identify patients who are becoming addicted.

"When it comes to people who don't have chronic pain and they're addicted, it's more straightforward because they're using some of these drugs as party drugs, things like that and the criteria for addiction are pretty clear," says Weiss.

"I think where it gets really complicated is when you've got somebody that's in chronic pain and they wind up needing higher and higher doses, and you don't know if this is a sign that they're developing problems of addiction because something is really happening in their brain that's . . . getting them more compulsively involved in taking the drug, or if their pain is getting worse because their disease is getting worse, or because they're developing tolerance to the painkiller," Weiss says.

"We know that drugs have risk, and what we're good at in medicine is recognizing risk and managing it, as long as we're willing to rise to that occasion," says Fishman. "The key is that one has to manage the risks."

3. Myth: Because most people don't get addicted to painkillers, I can use them as I please.

Reality: You need to use prescription painkillers (and any other drug) properly. It's not something patients should tinker with themselves.

"They definitely have an addiction potential," says Gharibo. His advice: Use prescription pain medicines as prescribed by your doctor and report your responses—positive and negative—to your doctor.

Gharibo also says that he doesn't encourage using opioids alone, but as part of a plan that also includes other treatment—including other types of drugs, as well as physical therapy and psychotherapy, when needed.

Gharibo says he tells patients about drugs' risks and benefits, and if he thinks an opioid is appropriate for the patient, he prescribes it on a trial basis to see how the patient responds. And although you may find that you need a higher dose, you shouldn't take matters into your own hands. Overdosing is a risk, so setting your dose isn't a do-it-yourself task.

"I think the escalation of the dosage is key," says Seppala. "If people find that they just keep adding to the dose, whether it's legitimate for pain or not, it's worth taking a look at what's going on, especially if they're not talking with the caregiver as they do that."

4. Myth: It's better to bear the pain than to risk addiction.

Reality: Undertreating pain can cause needless suffering. If you have pain, talk to your doctor about it, and if you're afraid about addiction, talk with them about that, too.

Addiction vs. Physical Dependence

Prescription painkillers are powerful drugs that reduce pain. These drugs are very helpful to people with severe pain from injuries, and cancer and other diseases.

Prescription painkillers attach to particular sites in the brain called opioid receptors, which carry messages about pain. With proper use of prescription painkillers, the pain messages sent to the brain are changed and are no longer perceived as painful. Patients who are pre- scribed painkillers for a long period of time may develop a "physical dependence" on them. This is not the same as addiction. Physical dependence happens because the body adapts to having the drug around, and when its use is stopped abruptly, the person can experience symptoms of withdrawal. That is why these drugs are carefully moni- tored and should be taken or stopped only under a doctor's orders.

Prescription painkillers can be highly addictive when used improperly—without a doctor's prescription or in doses higher than prescribed. Addiction means that a person will strongly crave the drug and continue to use it despite severe consequences to their health and their life. Prescription painkillers also affect the brain areas con- trolling respiration, and when used improperly (or mixed with other drugs), can cause a severe decrease in breath- ing that can lead to death.

"Mind Over Matter: Prescription Drug Abuse,"
NIDA for Teens, 2012. http://teens.drugabuse.gov.

"People have a right to have their pain addressed," says Fishman. "When someone's in pain, there's no risk-free op- tion, including doing nothing."

Fishman remembers a man who came to his emergency room with pain from prostate cancer that had spread throughout his body. "He was on no pain medicine at all," Fishman recalls.

Fishman wrote the man a prescription for morphine, and the next day, the man was out golfing. "But a week later, he was back in the emergency room with pain out of control," says Fishman. "He stopped taking his morphine because he thought anyone who took morphine for more than a week was an addict. And he was afraid that he was going to start robbing liquor stores and stealing lottery tickets. So these are very pervasive beliefs."

Weiss, who has seen her mother-in-law resist taking opioids to treat chronic pain, notes that some people suffer pain because they fear addiction, while others are too casual about using painkillers.

"We don't want to make people afraid of taking a medication that they need," says Weiss. "At the same time, we want people to take these drugs seriously."

5. Myth: All that matters is easing my pain.

Reality: Pain relief is key, but it's not the only goal.

"We're focusing on functional restoration when we prescribe analgesics or any intervention to control the patient's pain," says Gharibo.

He explains that functional restoration means "being autonomous, being able to attend to their activities of daily living, as well as forming friendships and an appropriate social environment."

In other words, pain relief isn't enough.

"If there is pain reduction without improved function, that may not be sufficient to continue opioid pharmacotherapy," says Gharibo. "If we're faced with a situation where we continue to increase the doses and we're not getting any functional improvement, we're not just going to go up and up on the dose. We're going to change the plan."

6. Myth: I'm a strong person. I won't get addicted.

Reality: Addiction isn't about willpower, and it's not a moral failure. It's a chronic disease, and some people are genetically more vulnerable than others, notes Fishman.

"The main risk factor for addiction is genetic predisposition," Seppala agrees. "Do you have a family history of alcohol or addiction? Or do you have a history yourself and now you're in recovery from that? That genetic history would potentially place you at higher risk of addiction for any substance, and in particular, you should be careful using the opioids for any length of time."

Seppala says prescription painkiller abuse was "rare" when his career began, but is now second only to marijuana in terms of illicit use.

Exactly how many people are addicted to prescription painkillers isn't clear. But 1.7 million people age 12 and older in the U.S. abused or were addicted to pain relievers in 2007, according to government data.

And in a 2007 government survey, about 57% of people who reported taking pain relievers for "nonmedical" uses in the previous month said they'd gotten pain pills for free from someone they knew; only 18% said they'd gotten it from a doctor.

Don't share prescription pain pills and don't leave them somewhere that people could help themselves. "These are not something that you should hand out to your friends or relatives or leave around so that people can take a few from you without your even noticing it," says Weiss.

7. Myth: My doctor will steer me clear of addiction.

Reality: Doctors certainly don't want their patients to get addicted. But they may not have much training in addiction, or in pain management.

Most doctors don't get much training in either topic, says Seppala. "We've got a naive physician population providing pain care and not knowing much about addiction. That's a bad combination."

Fishman agrees and urges patients to educate themselves about their prescriptions and to work with their doctors. "The best relationships are the ones where you're partnering with your clinicians and exchanging ideas."

> *"The misuse and intentional abuse of a diverse range of prescription medications has become a significant health threat and entrenched consumer behavior in American society."*

Ready Access to Prescription Drugs at Home Leads Many Teens to Abuse Them

Sean Clarkin

Sean Clarkin is the executive vice president of the Partnership at Drugfree.org. In the following viewpoint, he maintains that the abuse of prescription drugs by teenagers is a growing and serious problem in the United States. Clarkin outlines a number of contributing factors to the trend, including the fact that these substances are readily accessible to teens. Studies show, he contends, that dangerous and addictive prescription drugs can be found for free in the medicine cabinets of parents and friends. He describes recent efforts by his organization to educate parents of teens about the need to monitor their medications and to dispose of them properly when they are no longer needed. Additional cam-

Sean Clarkin, "Warning: The Growing Danger of Prescription Drug Diversion," Testimony Before the Subcommittee on Commerce, Manufacturing, and Trade, US House of Representatives, April 14 2011.

paigns are needed, according to Clarkin, to raise awareness of the problem and to change the attitudes and behaviors of teens, parents, policy makers, and prescribers.

As you read, consider the following questions:

1. According to the 2010 Partnership Attitude Tracking Study cited by Clarkin, what percentage of American teens reported taking a prescription drug not prescribed for them by a doctor at least once?

2. According to the National Survey on Drug Use and Health (NSDUH) cited in the viewpoint, what percentage of drug abusers say that they got drugs from family or friends?

3. What percentage of parents say that they had given their teenaged child a prescription drug without having a prescription for it, according to the viewpoint?

The Partnership at Drugfree.org is a nonprofit organization that helps parents prevent, intervene in and find treatment for drug and alcohol abuse by their children. My testimony today [in April 2011] will be focused on teens and young adults since that population is the focus of the Partnership's work.

When the Partnership addresses prescription drug abuse, we also consider over-the-counter cough and cold remedies which some teens use to get high. The abuse of prescription medications and over-the-counter remedies are both examples of beneficial medications being used in risky, unhealthy ways. Because today's hearing is focused on the diversion of prescription drugs, I will restrict my remarks to the nonmedical use of Rx [prescription] medications.

The abuse of prescription medications—legal substances of tremendous benefit if used appropriately—is the single most troubling phenomenon on today's drug landscape. The misuse and intentional abuse of a diverse range of prescription medications has become a significant health threat and entrenched consumer behavior in American society.

According to the 2010 Partnership Attitude Tracking Study—or "PATS" study—sponsored by the MetLife Foundation, teen abuse of Rx medicines continues to be an area of major concern, with abuse rates holding steady at levels that should be worrisome to parents. The data found one in four teens (25 percent) reported taking a prescription drug not prescribed for them by a doctor at least once in their lives, and more than one in five teens (23 percent) used a prescription pain reliever not prescribed for them by a doctor.

Contributing Factors to Teen Prescription Drug Abuse

Why have we as a nation not been able to reduce this risky behavior? There are several reasons:

Access

1. *Access.* These substances are readily available to teens—in their own medicine cabinets and the medicine cabinets of friends—and very often they are available for free. The Partnership's data are similar to the findings of the National Survey on Drug Use and Health (NSDUH) which shows that over 70% of prescription drug abusers say that they got those drugs from family or friends. In addition, nearly half (47%) of teens in our PATS survey say that it is easy to get these drugs from parents' medicine cabinets and more than a third (38%) say it is available everywhere.

That is why the Partnership worked with Abbott [Laboratories] to create Not in My House, a website to educate parents of teens about the need to monitor their medications, safeguard them and dispose of them properly when no longer needed.

It is also why we strongly supported the Drug Enforcement Administration's [DEA's] first prescription drug "Take-Back" day last fall—where they collected 121 tons of pills from 4,000 locations in 50 states—and why we are supporting their next "Take-Back" day on April 30. If we are able to get people to properly dispose of unneeded medications, we can make a significant dent in the supply of prescription medications that are being abused.

The proliferation of "pill mills" in certain areas of the country—where, for a price, individuals are able to obtain prescriptions for controlled substances without legitimate medical need—is a growing concern. Closing pill mills, having interoperable prescription monitoring programs to curtail doctor shopping, and educating prescribers about both addiction and pain management would likely go a long way toward reducing the supply of these medications in America's medicine cabinets.

Perception of Risk

2. *Perception of Risk.* Teens' perception of the risks associated with abusing prescription drugs is relatively low. Partnership research shows that less than half of teens see "great risk" in trying prescription pain relievers such as Vicodin or OxyContin that a doctor did not prescribe for them. The University of Michigan's "Monitoring the Future" survey data going back over thirty years demonstrates that teens' perception of the risk associated with any substance of abuse, along with perceptions of "social disapproval," correlates significantly with actual teen abuse of that substance. Low perception of risk, coupled with easy availability, is a recipe for an ongoing problem.

Motivations

3. *Motivations.* Research conducted by the Partnership in 2007, with support from Abbott, cast new light on the motivations

of teens to abuse prescription drugs. We have traditionally thought of teens abusing illegal drugs and alcohol either to "party," or to "self-medicate" for some serious problem or disorder: adolescent depression, for example.

But our 2007 research, like the research done among college students by Carol Boyd and Sean McCabe at the University of Michigan, suggests a wider range of motivations for young people's abuse of prescription drugs, including an emerging set of "life management" or "regulation" objectives. Teens appear to be abusing these drugs in a utilitarian way, using stimulants to help them cram for a test or lose weight, pain relievers to escape some of the pressure they feel to perform academically and socially, tranquilizers to wind down at the end of a stressful day. Once these substances have been integrated into teens' lives and abused as study or relaxation aids, it may become increasingly difficult to persuade teens that these drugs are unnecessary or unsafe when taken without a prescription.

This research also showed that prescription drug abuse is not a "substitute" behavior. That is to say, teens generally do not use prescription medication to get high *instead* of taking another substance. What we have found is that prescription drugs may act as a kind of "bridge" between the use of alcohol and marijuana, which many teens see as relatively benign substances, and harder "scarier" drugs such as cocaine.

Parents Are Key in Preventing Drug Abuse

4. *Parents.* Parents—who are usually our most valuable ally in preventing teen drug use—are generally ill-equipped to deal with teens' abuse of prescription drug use, a behavior that was probably not on their radar when they were teenagers. They find it hard to understand the scale and purposefulness with which today's teens are abusing medications, and it's not immediately clear to them that the prime source of supply for abusable prescription drugs is likely to be their own medicine

cabinet. Further, many parents themselves are misusing, or perhaps abusing, prescription drugs without having a prescription. In our study with Abbott, 28% of parents said they had used a prescription drug without having a prescription for it, and 8% of parents said they had given their teenaged child an Rx drug that was not prescribed for the teen. Our recent PATS study revealed that 22% of parents said there were situations where it would be OK for a parent to give a teen a prescription drug not prescribed for him or her.

Our 2010 PATS study also showed that teens continue to report that their parents do not talk to them about the risks of prescription drugs at the same levels of other substances of abuse. Fewer than one in four teens reported that a parent had discussed the risks of taking a prescription pain reliever (23%) or any prescription drug (22%) without a doctor's prescription. Contrast that to the relatively high number of teens who say their parents have discussed the risks of alcohol (81%) and marijuana (77%).

Much more work needs to be done to motivate parents to discuss the risks of prescription drug abuse with their teens. Partnership research through the years has demonstrated that kids who learn a lot at home about the risks of abusing drugs are half as likely to use. Encouraging these conversations and ongoing parental monitoring is key to reducing teen Rx abuse.

Prevention Efforts Need to Be Increased

5. *Need to Do More.* Finally, the reason why we have not yet been able to reduce teen abuse of prescription medications is that our efforts as a nation have been inadequate, at least to date. There has simply not been sufficient public attention or resources devoted to this threat.

The backdrop to all of this is that the national drug prevention infrastructure has been eroding for the past few years as the budget for the National Youth Anti-Drug Media Cam-

Trends in Teen Drug Use

Prescription drugs, when used as prescribed, can be powerful and effective medicines. However, many teens are abusing prescription drugs to get high.

In fact, more teens abuse prescription drugs than any illicit drug except marijuana—more than cocaine, heroin, and methamphetamine combined, according to the 2006 National Survey on Drug Use and Health (NSDUH). More than 2.1 million teens ages 12 to 17 reported abusing prescription drugs in 2006. Among 12- and 13-year-olds, prescription drugs are their drug of choice (NSDUH, 2007).

Prescription painkillers like Vicodin and OxyContin are the most often abused prescription drugs (NSDUH, 2007). The most recent Monitoring the Future (MTF) survey found that past-year abuse of Vicodin is particularly high among 8th, 10th, and 12th graders, with nearly one in 10 high school seniors reporting taking it in the past year without a doctor's approval (MTF, 2007). And the trend is growing; over a five-year period (2002–2007), past-year use of OxyContin increased by 30 percent (MTF, 2007).

"Teen Prescription Drug Abuse: An Emerging Threat,"
Community Anti-Drug Coalitions of America (CADCA),
January 2008.

paign has shrunk significantly, the Safe and Drug-Free Schools and Communities state grant program has been eliminated, and changes have been proposed to the state prevention and treatment block grant that could put prevention funding in jeopardy. With dwindling resources, it is impossible for government alone to mount the kind of effort that is needed to turn the tide on this problem.

Director [Gil] Kerlikowske, Administrator [Michele] Leon-hart, Commissioner [Margaret] Hamburg, Director [Nora] Volkow and others have done an excellent job of calling attention to this problem, both within government and among the public. Director Kerlikowske identified Rx abuse as one of his top three priorities and he has been working with all of the national drug control agencies to develop a targeted strategy to address the problem; the DEA prescription drug "Take-Back" days have begun the essential task of educating the public that old unneeded medication must not remain in the medicine cabinet; the FDA [Food and Drug Administration] is putting the spotlight on this issue as part of the Safe Use Initiative; and NIDA [National Institute on Drug Abuse] is engaged in targeted research, education and outreach that will be critical to curbing this behavior. The Community Anti-Drug Coalitions of America and the Treatment Research Institute are also doing important work in this area and should be commended for their efforts.

Awareness Campaigns

We know that when there is a well-funded effort to educate parents about the dangers of Rx abuse, we can increase awareness. In the first half of 2008 ONDCP's [Office of National Drug Control Policy's] National Youth Anti-Drug Media Campaign devoted $14 million (a $28 million value with the media match) to a parent-targeted campaign aimed at raising awareness about the risks of Rx abuse and motivating parents to take action. The campaign, which ran from February to July 2008, yielded significant and impressive results: parent perceptions about the prevalence of teen Rx abuse increased 10 percent and belief that it is a serious problem among teens jumped 17 percent. The likelihood that parents would take action also changed significantly: the number of parents who said that they would safeguard drugs at home increased 13%; monitor prescription medications and control access increased

12%; properly dispose of medications went up by 9%; and set clear rules about all drugs, including not sharing medications was up by 6%.

This shows that a major public education campaign can help to turn the tide on this entrenched behavior. The ONDCP [National Youth Anti-Drug] Media Campaign's funding is in jeopardy and may even be eliminated in the coming year so we cannot assume that it will be able to help deliver this message. The private sector—pharmaceutical companies, generic drug manufacturers, wholesalers, distributors, retailers, etc.— will need to help finance a campaign of the magnitude necessary to change the attitudes that underlie the behavior of nonmedical use of prescription medicine.

A number of individual pharmaceutical companies have stepped forward to work with the Partnership and other national organizations. Purdue Pharma funded some of our initial research to get our arms around this problem in 2004. They have also helped to fund a number of the parent intervention and treatment resources at drugfree.org as well as some of our community education efforts. Abbott underwrote the in-depth consumer research conducted in 2007 to assess the attitudes and beliefs underlying the behavior of prescription drug abuse. We also worked with them to create Not in My House, a website designed to educate parents of teens to monitor their medications, secure them properly and properly dispose of them when no longer needed.

Working Together to Address Prescription Drug Abuse

While we are grateful for the efforts of our partner companies, if our nation is going to reduce teen abuse of prescription medication we need to step up efforts dramatically. We need a sustained, multiyear effort funded by the pharmaceutical industry, the generic drug manufacturers and other key stakeholders to:

1. support a major, independent paid media campaign alerting consumers to the risks of abusing medicine and the importance of safeguarding and safely disposing of medicine. This effort might include tagging the pharmaceutical industry's large inventory of direct-to-consumer advertising and pointing viewers toward an objective and comprehensive online prevention resource;

2. educate and enlist prescribers, pharmacists and other health care professionals about addiction and pain management;

3. coordinate outreach by employees of all the relevant stakeholder companies and other interested parties to increase awareness about Rx abuse and disposal at the local level;

4. educate policy makers at the local, state and federal level about this problem so that we can promote policies that will help reduce both the supply of and demand for prescription drugs to abuse; and

5. implement an evaluation tool that will measure and hold the program accountable.

Moving Forward

We believe that the abuse of prescription medications—legal substances of great benefit when used properly—is the single most troubling phenomenon on today's drug abuse landscape. We remain committed to a long-term effort to educate the public on the risks of intentional medicine abuse and to reducing the level of abuse in society. We have laid important groundwork in this area but feel that there needs to be a major paid media and public relations campaign over the next five years in order to change the relevant attitudes and behavior of not only teens but also parents, policy makers, and prescribers. This effort must be focused not only on raising awareness about the risks of taking medications without a doctor's prescription but it must also be a call to action to all adults to take responsibility for what is in their medicine cabinets and dispose of unneeded prescriptions in a timely manner.

This education campaign needs to be accompanied by coordinated community education efforts and public policy changes. And, of course, it should be rigorously evaluated.

The misuse and intentional abuse of a diverse range of prescription medications has become a significant health threat and entrenched consumer behavior in American society.

We appreciate the time and attention that the Subcommittee [on Commerce, Manufacturing, and Trade of the US House of Representatives] is giving to raising awareness and looking for ways to reduce the abuse of prescription drugs in our country. The Partnership at Drugfree.org stands ready to work with the subcommittee on this and other substance abuse matters.

> *"Drug companies hire 'detail' men and women to visit physician offices to sell their latest products and provide 'drug education' materials to doctors—all of this to make drug manufacturing . . . profitable."*

Pharmaceutical Companies Encourage Physicians to Overprescribe Drugs

Ellen Ratner

Ellen Ratner is the Washington bureau chief for the Talk Radio News Service. In the following viewpoint, she opines that physicians are too eager to prescribe drugs to treat patients rather than pursue other, more natural solutions. Ratner asserts that the pharmaceutical companies have spent millions of dollars to lobby Congress and government agencies to suppress information on adult prescription drug abuse. Also, she contends, drug companies have pressured doctors to prescribe their medications and medical schools to abandon integrative methods as well as other natural therapies and medical strategies. As a result, Ratner concludes, prescription drugs are overprescribed and other remedies are never explored, despite what is best for the patient.

As you read, consider the following questions:

1. How does Ratner describe the philosophy of Dr. Mel Pohl?

2. What finally alleviated Ratner's anxiety, according to the viewpoint?

3. According to Ratner, what percentage do drug companies make in profit every year?

Many issues that columnists write about stem from personal experience, and this column is no exception. Recently, I succumbed to the mental state that seems to be an old friend of my extended family members: anxiety. It has not bothered me for almost 20 years but revisited me in full force this winter.

A Troubling Episode

I received a recommendation and went to visit my friendly neighborhood psychopharmacologist who, despite my objections, prescribed one of the new benzodiazepines (a class of drugs that includes Valium, Librium, Klonopin). I explained to him that I had worked in the field of addictions for many years and that it was not a class of drugs with which I am comfortable. I then produced a list of vitamins and supplements given to me by my general physician and asked if they were good or if I should be taking more, less or different ones. I got a nice smile and a blank stare. This guy was well educated and young, so, presumably, he was not stuck in old patterns.

Against my better judgment, I took the pills and got temporary relief. But I was uncomfortable and did not react well to them. So, I decided to brave it, put up with the anxiety and hope for the best. During this time, my old friend, Dr. Mel Pohl, released a book titled *A Day Without Pain*. Mel is an internist who specializes in addiction and pain management, and this is his latest book. He believes that people become too addicted to legal, prescribed drugs and that there are many other ways to treat pain without whipping out the prescription pad. I read Mel's book and decided that the psychopharmacologist who had suggested that I take the benzodiazepines was buying into the drug companies' sales pitch, hook, line and sinker. (To be sure, there is a time and place for medication, especially with psychotic disorders.)

Integrative Medicine

I searched for a physician who worked with mind/body alternatives and understood what is now being called "integrative medicine." I quickly found someone who uses many different methods including breathing techniques, vitamins and herbs, biofeedback and other methods and reserves the prescription pad for backup. In two office visits during a period of three weeks, I felt better than I had in months. I had no drugs, just natural techniques and supplements that worked with my body rhythms.

Being a journalist and considering writing an article about this, I decided to do some online research about the overprescribing of drugs. What I found—or actually to be more precise, what I did not find—was shocking.

What I Found

There is a huge lack of anything devoted to adult prescription drug abuse from our government. There is a ton of information and research on taxpayer-funded websites about teenage abuse of prescription drugs, but the lack of information on adult misuse of legal drugs is astounding. You don't have to be a Las Vegas poker player to speculate why, either. It is lobbying on Capitol Hill by the drug companies. It is also the not-so-subtle brainwashing of America's physicians from medical school to practice that is taking place every day in

"What does Perkemup do? What would you like it to do?!" Cartoon by Mark Dubowski. www.CartoonStock.com.

schools, hospitals and offices. Everyone agrees kids should not be using drugs to abuse them, but it is fashionable to look the other way with adults.

The Role of Pharmaceutical Companies

Time and time again, the drug company lobbyists have graced our presence in Washington with their full-fledged army and money assault. We saw them like ants on a sugar cube during

Medicare Part B. They even walked a few blocks and have made themselves known to staffers at the Department of Health and Human Services to try and dissuade the breast-feeding campaign in favor of infant formula.

The drug companies hire "detail" men and women to visit physician offices to sell their latest products and provide "drug education" materials to the doctors—all of this to make drug manufacturing one of the recession-proof profitable businesses on the planet, garnering up to about 18 percent a year in profit. The medical schools that often rely on the drug companies' payments for research are not about to make alternative and integrative medicine a major part of the curriculum. Sure, you might see a course in it, but it does not take a starring role on any exams or anything else that really matters in a young doctor's education.

Why? It serves all interested parties. The drug companies sell lots of drugs, the psychiatrists have relatively healthy non-nuisance neurotic patients that come back to them for another hit of drugs, and the patients do not have to do much homework such as breathing or body work. Everyone is satisfied in this arrangement, but no one gets healed. Maybe two of the three parties get rich, but the patients' health fails to improve.

> "When the situation is considered ratio-
> nally, our outsized fear of addiction has
> little to do with the reality of chronic
> pain. Instead, it's about the way we see
> addicts ... [as] people we don't want
> to be around or become."

Physicians and Pharmaceutical Companies Should Not Be Blamed for Drug Abuse

Maia Szalavitz

Maia Szalavitz is an author, a columnist at The Fix, *and a health reporter at* Time *magazine online. In the following viewpoint, she suggests that attempts to fight prescription drug abuse should not be targeting pharmaceutical companies that are manufacturing the next generation of prescription painkillers, the physicians who have been intimidated and harassed by law enforcement, or legitimate patients who need opioid painkillers to treat chronic pain. Szalavitz contends that Americans have let their fears of addiction and hard-core drug addicts create a stigma against prescription drugs. Instead of blaming doctors for addiction, she concludes it is time to blame the addicts who fail to take medication as prescribed or lie to obtain a prescription.*

Maia Szalavitz, "America's Exploding Oxy Epidemic," *The Fix*, June 17, 2011. Copyright © 2011 by The Fix. All rights reserved. Reproduced by permission.

As you read, consider the following questions:

1. According to Institute of Medicine estimates cited in the viewpoint, how many Americans suffer with moderate to severe chronic pain?

2. What has been the rate of Americans addicted to Oxy-Contin, Vicodin, Percocet, and other prescription drugs since 2002, according to government statistics cited by Szalavitz?

3. What drug does Szalavitz believe should be prescribed by doctors to prevent opioid poisoning?

Is addiction a fate worse than unremitting, agonizing pain? To many people, the answer is absolutely not—particularly if the sufferer is close to death. But that's not how our policy makers—and even many people affected by addiction—seem to view the issue.

While use of prescription opioids for cancer and other end-of-life pain is increasingly accepted, if you are going to suffer in agony for years, rather than months, mercy is harder to find. Indeed, it seems a given by the media that because addicts *sometimes* fake pain to get drugs, doctors should treat *all* patients as likely liars—and if a physician is conned by an addict, the doctor has only herself to blame.

Questions Raised by Legislating Chronic Pain Treatment

But do we really want our doctors to treat us as if we were guilty until proven innocent? Do we really want the routine use of invasive procedures—ranging from nerve conduction tests to repeated scans and surgeries—to "prove" we're really hurting? And do we actually want physicians to be held responsible for the actions of a patient who dissembles and does not take drugs as prescribed?

The answers to these questions are at the heart of the bizarre way we view synthetic opioid medications and the suffering of the 116 million Americans who have moderate to severe chronic pain, according to Institute of Medicine estimates.

In recent weeks, for example, New York Sen. Charles Schumer, anti–drug abuse advocates and reporters have inveighed against the potential FDA [Food and Drug Administration] approval of an experimental opioid painkiller called Zohydro—professing to be horrified by the introduction of a new class of "100% pure" hydrocodone "superdrugs" that they have already dubbed "the next OxyContins." And many states are weighing laws like one now in place in Washington State, which limits the doses of opioids that can be used by chronic pain patients.

Stoking Addiction Fears

When people consider the use of these medications in chronic pain, addiction fears are typically the first thing that comes up. Moreover, media coverage rarely includes the perspective of pain patients—or does so only to knock those who advocate for access to opioids as pawns of the pharmaceutical industry.

If the press—often quoting leading public health officials like Dr. Thomas Frieden, the director of the CDC [Centers for Disease Control and Prevention]—is to be believed, the US is in the throes of an "epidemic" of prescription painkiller abuse. Frieden even claimed at a recent press conference on opioid-related deaths that doctors are now more responsible than drug dealers for America's addiction problems. "The burden of dangerous drugs is being created more by a few irresponsible doctors than drug pushers on street corners," Friedman said.

A Dissenting View

However, the opioid issue looks very different when you examine the numbers closely. For one, the rates of Americans addicted to OxyContin, Vicodin, Percocet, fentanyl and other products in our synthetic narcotic medicine cabinet are not rising. In fact, they have been steady at 0.8% since 2002, according to the government's own statistics.

Moreover, fewer than 1% of people over 30 (without a prior history of serious drug problems) become an addict while taking opioids; for chronic pain patients who are not screened for a history of previous drug problems, the addiction rate is 3.27%. That means, of course, that more than 96% do not become addicted.

Yet these statistics usually go unmentioned in media accounts because they do not confirm the preferred panic narrative. Also left out is the fact that around 80% of Oxy addicts (a) did not obtain the drug via legitimate prescription for pain and/or (b) had a prior experience of rehab. Their contact with the medical system—if any—was not what caused their addictions.

The Truth About Prescription Drug Addiction

So, the first thing the public really needs to know about what doctors call "iatrogenic addiction" is that it is extremely rare. If you've made it out of your 20s without becoming an addict, the chances that you will get hooked on pain treatment are miniscule—and even young people are not at high risk in most medical settings.

Nonetheless, the media continue to love them some "innocent victims"—and the real story of not-so-blameless drug users who move from heavy drinking, cocaine use and marijuana smoking to prescription drug abuse is just not as compelling. This, sadly, only contributes to the delusion that anyone who is treated for chronic pain with opioids is at risk for drowning in the—gasp!—ubiquitous riptide of addiction.

The panic leads to policies that require pain patients to be urine tested, to be called in to their doctors' offices for random "pill counts" and to make frequent visits—all of which is not only humiliating but expensive and time-consuming. There's little evidence that such policing prevents addiction or does anything else beyond inconveniencing and stigmatizing pain patients.

The Stigma of Addiction

And indeed, the stigma of addiction is what's behind the curtain here. Imagine suffering from incurable daily pain so severe that it feels like your legs are being dipped in molten iron or your spine is being scraped out by sharp talons. Even if you did, in a worst-case scenario, join the tiny percentage of patients who develop a new addiction and became obsessed with using opioids, would this really be worse, especially if you had safe and legal access to them?

Most of the physical and psychological horrors of addiction come with loss of control and with being unable to be present for family, work and friends. But pain can produce even greater dysfunction and emotional distance, and its ability to destroy relationships is at least as monstrous. Moreover, maintenance on opioids can typically stabilize people with addictions, without numbing or incapacitating them. So why do we panic?

In the absence of true pharmaceutical innovation (Zohydro and other "superdrugs" are mere purer versions of Vicodin without the acetaminophen), opioids remain the only medications that can even begin to touch severe pain, though they are far from perfect. But since they rarely lead to addiction— and since addiction (or opioid maintenance treatment) may actually sometimes be the lesser of evils—does it really make sense to restrict and even deny their benefits to pain patients?

When the situation is considered rationally, our outsized fear of addiction has little to do with the reality of chronic pain. Instead, it's about the way we see addicts: gun-toting robbers of Oxy from pharmacies and other scummy, lying, sociopathic criminals—people we don't want to be around or become.

Even though readers of this site [*The Fix* blog] know that drugs don't somehow "make" ordinary people into such demonic figures—and that addicts can also be as kind, compassionate and hardworking as anyone else—the stigma runs deep.

What Happened to Personal Responsibility?

Much of it, I think, comes from the same evasion of responsibility that allows us to blame doctors for addictions. After all, it's not doctors who tell their patients to inject or snort their oral painkillers, to drink while taking opioids, to take more than prescribed or to lie, cheat and steal to obtain them.

These actions are deliberately taken by drug seekers. Doctors don't "make" anyone make the ongoing choices that lead to impaired self-control. While trauma histories, psychiatric disorders like depression and/or genetics do make some of us more vulnerable to taking this path, no one can force us to do it. And if we see doctors—or, for that matter, dealers—as having "caused" our addictions, we open ourselves up to be dehumanized and stigmatized.

That is because if we are seen as incapable of making good choices, how can we expect respect for our desires and preferences? If we can't control ourselves, why shouldn't we be incarcerated to protect others from our actions? After all, when the public sees us as mindless zombies, their response is not sympathy for our supposed powerlessness but fear and disgust at our imagined violence.

Even the overdose issue is mismanaged due to our hatred of addicts. Overdoses have now overtaken car accidents as a leading cause of accidental death, but it's unclear how much of this increase is due to the actual rise in the use of opioids and how much to medical examiners simply attributing more deaths to these drugs since they are now found in more dead people. What *is* clear is that most of these deaths occur in the context of drug abuse—95%, according to one study of one of the hardest-hit states. A large number of these deaths could be prevented by providing the antidote to opioid poisoning, naloxone, with prescriptions for the drugs. But because we want the wages of sin to be death, however, drug warriors have largely prevented funding for programs to broadly distribute that lifesaving medication.

The opioid problem is really the stigma of addiction writ large. Consequently, if we want to stop getting in the way of access to painkillers for people who genuinely need them, we need to take responsibility for our own actions and help fight this stigma. No one but you can make yourself into an addict. But chronic pain can happen to anyone.

> "*Antianxiety drugs are the salvation of those for whom opting out of the to-do list isn't an option.*"

Prescription Drug Abuse Is a By-Product of Modern American Life

Lisa Miller

Lisa Miller is a writer and journalist. In the following viewpoint, she views the abuse of prescription drugs, particularly antianxiety medication like Xanax and Prozac, as a by-product of the fast-paced and economically uncertain nature of modern American life in the twenty-first century. As Americans strive to succeed in a competitive marketplace and are beset by political and economic worries, Miller contends, antianxiety drugs take the edge off and allow sleep and moments of calm. Miller explains that those medications also treat conditions like low-grade depression, panic disorder, phobias, post-traumatic stress disorder (PTSD), obsessive-compulsive disorder (OCD), and situational anxiety, which can be caused by a specific event such as losing a job or experiencing financial difficulty. Miller notes that there is a general ambivalence to the use of antianxiety drugs, but such drugs remain a popular trend across a number of demographic groups. Unfortunately, she writes, these drugs are extremely addictive and are frequently abused.

As you read, consider the following questions:

1. According to Miller, how many prescriptions were written for a generic form of Xanax in 2010?
2. When does Miller say that Miltown was discovered?
3. What was the first drug to reach $100 million in sales, according to the viewpoint?

"I use my anxiety to be better at what I do," says an executive at a boutique PR [public relations] firm. "A certain amount of anxiety makes me a better employee but a less happy person, and you have to constantly balance that. If I didn't constantly fear I was about to be fired or outed as a loser, I'm afraid I might be lazy." She takes a melt-in-your mouth .25-milligram tab of Klonopin once a week, she estimates: at bedtime, if work stress has her too revved up, or on the subway in the morning if her schedule for the day is making her sweat. Antianxiety drugs are the salvation of those for whom opting out of the to-do list isn't an option.

"Benzos"

Xanax and its siblings—Valium, Ativan, Klonopin, and other members of the family of drugs called benzodiazepines—suppress the output of neurotransmitters that interpret fear. They differ from one another in potency and duration; those that enter your brain most quickly (Valium and Xanax) can make you the most high. But all quell the racing heart, spinning thoughts, prickly scalp, and hyperventilation associated with fear's neurotic cousin, anxiety, and all do it more or less instantly. Prescriptions for benzodiazepines have risen 17 percent since 2006 to nearly 94 million a year; generic Xanax, called alprazolam, has increased 23 percent over the same period, making it the most prescribed psychopharmaceutical drug and the eleventh most prescribed overall, with 46 million prescriptions written in 2010. In their generic forms, Xanax is prescribed more than the sleeping pill Ambien, more than the antidepressant Zoloft. Only drugs for chronic conditions like high blood pressure and high cholesterol do better.

"Benzos," says Stephen Stahl, chairman of the Neuroscience Education Institute in Carlsbad, California, and a psychiatrist who consults to drug companies, "are the greatest things since Post Toasties. They work well. They're very cheap. Their effectiveness on anxiety is profound."

Benzos can also be extremely addictive, and their popularity can be gauged by their illegitimate uses as well. According to the federal Substance Abuse and Mental Health Services Administration [SAMHSA], rehab visits involving benzodiazepine use tripled between 1998 and 2008. Though benzos have come to signify the frantic overwhelmed-ness of the professional elites (they were discovered in the autopsies of both Michael Jackson and Heath Ledger), SAMHSA says the person likeliest to abuse the drugs is a white man between the ages of 18 and 34 who is addicted to another substance—alcohol, heroin, painkillers—and is unemployed. Last year, a 27-year-old man named Dominick Glowacki demanded that a Westchester CVS hand over all its Xanax while he held up the store with a BB gun. Jeffrey Chartier, the Bronx lawyer who represented Glowacki, says he's seeing more and more cases of benzo abuse among young men who aren't working. "Two pills and two beers make them as high as drinking the whole six-pack."

In these anxious times, Xanax offers a lot. It dissolves your worries, whatever they are, like a special kiss from Mommy. "Often referred to as God's gift," reads the fifth definition of Xanax on Urban Dictionary. "You could come home with your house on fire and not even care," reads another. "You don't give a f*** about nothing." So reliably relaxing are the effects of benzodiazepines that SAMHSA's director of substance abuse treatment, H. Westley Clark, says they've gained a reputation as "alcohol in a pill." And their consumption can be equally informal. Just as friends pour wine for friends in times of crisis, so too do doctors, moved by the angst of their patients, "have sympathy and prescribe more," says Clark. There are a lot more benzos circulating these days, and a lot more sharing.

The Benefits of "Benzos"

In my social circle, benzodiazepines are traded with generosity and goodwill. My first Klonopin was given to me three years ago by a friend, during the third of seemingly endless rounds of layoffs. "You'll know it's working when you stop spinning," she told me as she dug for the foil packet in her purse. Another friend admitted she has recently found herself playing fairy godmother with her Xanax. To friends worried about enduring a family holiday, she doles out a pill; to colleagues fearful of flying, she'll commiserate before offering a cure. "I can't fly without half a Xanax," she'll say. "Want some?" (Such casual bigheartedness is perhaps abetted by how cheap alprazolam can be. "How's this for something nutty," the same friend wrote to me in an e-mail. "Just refilled alprazolam. It was $2.56 for 30 tabs. Less than pretty much anything in the drugstore except maybe gum or Blistex.")

The beauty of a benzo is its simplicity. SSRIs [selective serotonin reuptake inhibitors] like Prozac or Celexa can work on anxiety as well as depression, but take two to three weeks to kick in. A benzo is, plain and pure, a chill pill: You can take it when you need to without committing to months or years of talk therapy. A real estate executive I spoke to packs antianxiety drugs whenever he travels to guard against the circumstance he most dreads: being stuck in a hotel room (or, as he was recently, on a family camping trip), unable to sleep and worrying about not sleeping. "It's just one of my little neuroses," he says. He finds that as long as he has the pills on hand, he rarely has to use them. "Just knowing they're there makes me feel better."

I understand what he means. The Ativan I snagged from my mother is mostly untouched since she died six months ago. Benzos are great when you are freaking out—and they're great because you know that something will make you freak out, eventually.

The Miltown Phenomenon

The last antianxiety drug Americans loved as much as Xanax was called Miltown. Discovered by accident in 1955 by a researcher looking for a new muscle relaxant, it caught on almost overnight. In Hollywood and New York, where busy, glamorous people worked all hours to feed the masses' appetite for information and entertainment, hostesses served martinis with a Miltown garnish. Tiffany & Co. produced a line of tiny jeweled cases in which a woman might carry her pills. Lucille Ball, Lauren Bacall, Tennessee Williams, and Norman Mailer all took Miltown. Not only did they take it, but they boasted about the relief they felt from the miracle drug the press dubbed "Executive Excedrin." On his show, Bob Hope called Miltown the "I don't care" pill.

Against a backdrop of the real and present threat of nuclear attack, it would not be an exaggeration to say that during the Cold War it was patriotic to take an antianxiety drug. The medicine kept ambitious working people (mostly men) on an even keel while their children were ducking and covering at school. Miltown allowed Americans to manage the stresses of modernity while "doing one's job and earning a good salary, but also playing a social role: making decisions and completing tasks while maintaining confidence and control," writes Andrea Tone in her excellent book *The Age of*

Anxiety: A History of America's Turbulent Affair with Tranquilizers. It wasn't just that anxiety was normal. It wasn't normal if you weren't anxious.

Valium

Valium came along in 1963, developed by Roche to knock Miltown off its perch. Unlike Miltown, which was a word-of-mouth phenomenon, Valium was aggressively marketed as a consumer convenience. The target audience was women, whose grouchiness, stress, romantic woes, and mood swings the drug would cure. One 1970 ad showed "Mrs. Raymond," a schoolteacher, facing a relatable female crisis. "Valium has helped free her of the excessive psychic tension and associated depressive symptoms accompanying her menopause," it read. "Now she's poised and cheerful again."

Valium's success was unprecedented. It was the first drug, according to Tone, to reach $100 million in sales. It was also the first drug to trigger in Americans the suspicion that they were being sold a panacea for a condition they didn't have or that might otherwise be cured by fulfilling work, a good laugh, or a more empathetic husband.

Xanax: The Next Generation

Xanax, approved in 1981, was a massive technological improvement. Valium can linger in the system for as many as 100 hours and had gained a reputation for leaving its users hung over and zombified—"unable to feel warmth, unable to love, unable to cry, to taste, to smell," as Barbara Gordon put it in her 1989 memoir *I'm Dancing as Fast as I Can.* Xanax has a similar chemical composition but a much shorter half-life, vanishing hours after it takes effect. It gained a foothold in the antianxiety market as a spot treatment; it was indicated for "panic disorder," which had just been established as a legitimate pathology. But a growing number of Americans found that it worked on quotidian panic as well, the kind that comes with a child's disappointing, future-ruining report card or an intimate dinner party at the home of the person who signs your paychecks.

The Prozac Era

Benzodiazepines also got a boost from the Prozac era. Though new research has raised questions about their efficacy, SSRIs revolutionized the way people sought and received treatment for minor mental illnesses. Before Prozac, a person with low-grade depression or anxiety would turn to talk therapy, which was expensive, time-consuming, and not necessarily effective; another treatment was a family of drugs called tricyclics, which could have nasty side effects. After Prozac, that same person could take a much safer pill, and that pill could be procured with a simple visit to the family doctor. So even though doctors and drug makers continue to recommend drug therapy together with talk therapy, people with minor mental illness have over the past ten years increasingly sought help from drugs alone. A study published in the journal *Psychiatry* in 2008 showed that 55 percent of all prescriptions for benzodiazepines were written by general practitioners, and according to the National Institute of Mental Health [NIMH], people in treatment for psychological problems now spend half their budgeted dollars on drugs and less than a third on therapy. In 1997, those ratios were reversed.

Situational Anxiety

It may be that this moment in history justifies an increased use of benzos. Ronald Kessler, an epidemiologist at Harvard University, does sweeping, long-term studies for the National Institutes of Health. He has found that a quarter of Americans will have a diagnosed episode of anxiety—generalized anxiety disorder, panic, phobias, post-traumatic stress disorder, obsessive-compulsive disorder—in their lifetimes. That number, he says, hasn't changed in decades. But Kessler's research doesn't account for the blips he calls "situational anxiety," which come with tough times: an underwater mortgage, a diminished retirement account, or a child deployed in a foreign war. A benzodiazepine, says Kessler, could be a reasonable answer to "a terrible situation." Just as the exhausted new mother of a colicky 3-month-old might drink two cups of coffee in the morning instead of one, so might a banker facing the wrong end of a "strategic restructuring" pop a Xanax before an encounter with the boss. "This goes beyond the science," says Kessler, "but it could be that a pharmacological solution is the smart thing to do."

The question, then, is one of degree. The crises people face in these early months of 2012 are individual and circumstantial, yes, but they're global and abstract as well, stemming largely from the haunting awareness (it's certainly haunting me) that the fates of everyone in the world are intertwined and the job of protecting civilization from assorted inevitable disasters seems to have fallen to no one. "Situational anxiety" today stems from threats that are both everywhere and nowhere at once. How will the debtor nations in the eurozone ever manage to pay back what they owe? How can Israel disarm Iran's nuclear program without inciting the messiest international conflict since World War II? How can you be absolutely, 100 percent sure the cantaloupe you had for lunch wasn't contaminated with *Listeria* that will make you or your kids or one of your guests deathly sick?

To the point: Do modern realities merit an increased dependence on Xanax? Steven Hayes, a clinical psychologist at the University of Nevada, believes that benzos stop a gap that evolution has yet to fill. As humans try to control an exponentially growing number of inputs with which they are confronted, "our attention becomes less flexible, our minds become more chattering, and the next thing we know, we're frantic." Humans are ill-equipped to process or accommodate all these new signals. "Our task now is to create modern minds

What Is Xanax?

Xanax ([generic name:] alprazolam) belongs to a group of drugs called benzodiazepines. It works by slowing down the movement of chemicals in the brain that may become unbalanced. This results in a reduction in nervous tension (anxiety).

Xanax is used to treat anxiety disorders, panic disorders, and anxiety caused by depression.

"Xanax," Drugs.com, 2012.

for the modern world, and that modern mind has to be psychologically flexible." In the absence of that flexibility, Hayes says, people need a bridge—a pill—between what life doles out and what people can realistically handle.

Pharmacological Calvinism

In 1972, a psychiatrist named Gerald Klerman coined the phrase "pharmacological Calvinism" to describe Americans' tortured love affair with psychopharmaceutical drugs. Klerman was writing at the height of the Valium era, when its huge popularity lived alongside the perception, fed and perpetuated by the nascent feminist movement, that the pills were creating a generation of robot wives—numb, unfulfilled suburbanites forced into domestic servitude by the men who ran things, including the pharmaceutical companies. "You wake up in the morning," wrote Betty Friedan in *The Feminine Mystique*, "and you feel as if there's no point in going on another day like this. So you take a tranquilizer because it makes you not care so much that it's pointless." As fashionable as it was to take the pills, it was also fashionable to blame them.

On the one hand, Americans love convenience and scientific progress and thus herald drugs like Miltown and Xanax as miracle cures (like the washing machine or canned spaghetti) for the travails of modern life. On the other, Americans value self-reliance and authentic experience and regard dependency on chemicals as weak. Especially in this era, when entire sectors of the population have devoted themselves to eating organic and giving birth without painkillers, when otherwise sane parents decline to vaccinate their children against fatal diseases, chemical purity is held up as a sacred shield against future environmental cataclysm and failures of personal health.

Benzos sit at the locus of all this ambivalence, the love and the loathing often bumping awkwardly together within the same person. The same people who rely on Xanax, joke openly about it, and share it with friends who refuse to identify themselves on the record for fear of reprisal from colleagues and bosses (who, they tell me, are using it and joking about it as well). The same kinds of people who shop at the Park Slope Food Coop, that high temple of food purity, also take the occasional Xanax to chill out. "Coming to the co-op and doing something that is easy and meeting people actually helps me relax (no Xanax needed!)," one member opined about her work shift on Yelp. The inconsistency dwells even in my own self: As I write this story, I keep wanting to insist upon my physical and mental health and the lightness of my benzo habit. I spin, I do yoga, I eat lean meats and vegetables. I take half a tablet of Ativan every three weeks. At most. Honest.

A friend of mine had dental surgery recently, a procedure she both hates and fears. So proud was she that she'd sworn off Klonopin that she decided to forgo the medication ahead of her dental appointment. "I thought, *Don't be a baby. That's just weak. You should be able to handle things.*" She had a panic attack in the chair and was "a total bitch," she says, to the dentist. "Oh, wait a second," she reminded herself as the drill whined and the tooth dust spattered, "there's a medical reason for these things."

The Downside of "Benzo" Use

Psychologists wish people wouldn't take so many benzos and, especially, so much Xanax. "Surely it can't be right that this level of pharmaceuticals makes sense," says Hayes. Partly they say this out of professional obligation. Tone's book refers to Xanax as "the crack [cocaine] of the benzodiazepines." Its short half-life can mean disaster for people who use it daily: They crash as the drug is wearing off and immediately yearn for more. "The withdrawals are the worst (put me in the hospital)," reads a posting on a drug rehab website. "Find something else to do like pot or beer." Dr. Peter Breggin, who crusades against benzodiazepines, pointed out in an editorial in the *Huffington Post* after Whitney Houston died that even short-term use of Xanax can make people more anxious than they were before and that sporadic use can cause what he calls "medication spellbinding": impaired judgment, loss of memory and self-control. "I have all these mixed feelings about psychopharmaceuticals," says the friend who, like me, stole drugs from her deceased mother. "Messing with your brain chemistry isn't something to be taken lightly."

But the anti-benzo psychologists are also making a value judgment. They believe Americans would be better, and healthier, if they learned to manage their anxiety without pills. They believe people should feel their feelings. A pill can be a crutch, says Doug Mennin, an anxiety specialist at Hunter College who does private therapy for the functionally anxious. The more you use it, the less able you are to navigate life's tough spots on your own. "I'm a New Yorker," says Mennin. "I see dependency on pills all the time. What I say to clients is, 'You're selling yourself short a little bit.' If you're going through a stressful time, and you say, 'I'm going to get some of these,' then the next time you get to that kind of problem, you start seeking out that pill. If you didn't have the pill, you'd probably be okay." The mind is a muscle, Mennin adds. With practice, you can teach it to handle anxiety: "It's the same kind of skill as learning a better backhand in tennis."

Acceptance Therapy

Mennin, Hayes, and other anxiety researchers are excited about a new kind of treatment that seems to work even on therapy-resistant worriers. It's called "acceptance therapy" or "mindfulness therapy." Instead of trying to show a worrier how his anxiety is irrational, ill-founded, overblown, or corrosive to his physical health, intimate relationships, and personal happiness (the protocol in conventional therapies), the therapist instead endeavors to teach him to regard his anxiety with the cool dispassion of a Buddhist monk. Thus the patient doesn't get "entangled," as the shrinks say, with his anxiety. He doesn't try to flee from it. Nor does he try to evade or suppress it. He sees that it's there but resists the urge to respond to its call: to pick up the phone, turn on the computer, check the e-mail, eat that bag of cheese puffs, pour another drink, take that pill.

"If you can train people to be more in the present moment, they may be less worried about what could happen in the future. The idea is to be accepting of what your experience may be, whether it's anxiety or sadness or boredom," says Susan Evans, a professor of psychology and clinical psychiatry at Weill Cornell Medical College. "It may feel this way now, but it won't feel this way an hour from now, a day from now, a month from now." Evans teaches "mindfulness-based stress reduction" to groups on the Upper East Side. The cost of the training is $600 for eight two-hour sessions.

It turns out that I am afflicted not just with pharmacological Calvinism but with mindfulness skepticism as well. For while I believe, in theory, that learning to coolly regard my anxiety as a purple, hairy monster I could stash in my tote bag, as Mennin suggests, might steady my pulse on sleepless nights, I am suspicious of any cure that requires more effort and expense on my part and more hours away from my work and my family. In this skepticism, I am like my anxious peers. "We go through rough patches, and we do things that make us feel better," says Lisa Colpe, an epidemiologist at the NIMH, with the vocal equivalent of a shrug. A lot of people with anxiety would simply prefer to live with it; they know that when it becomes unbearable, the drugs will be there.

A cure isn't what the PR executive with the occasional Klonopin habit wants. "My own personal experience is that there's a healthy level of anxiety, and I don't believe 'healthy' is the absence of anxiety," she says. "I live in a world that puts unreasonable demands on me, and sometimes I need help. I wish I could do it without the pills, but I can't."

The real love affair, then, is not with the pills but with the anxiety itself. Anxiety is like the spouse you're stuck with for better and worse, who makes you nuts but has permeated your cells and without whom you cannot imagine your own heart beating. Anxiety lives with you day and night, holding your hand and nudging you to act, urging you to get up, do more, fix something, make something. Never satisfied, always pressing, it wants you to win, to outlast the others, to impress, excite, excel, astonish. And, as in a marriage, you comply, mostly agreeably, for your anxiety traces the rhythm of your life. Then one morning, it has you by the throat and you find yourself weepy and overwrought, unable to respond to its call. Like a reliable friend, Xanax is there, offering an intermission, the gift of quietude, a break. Because the truth is, and I'll speak for myself here, I want tranquillity once in a while. But I don't want a tranquil life.

Periodical and Internet Sources Bibliography

The following articles have been selected to supplement the diverse views presented in this chapter.

Radley Balko	"The War over Prescription Painkillers," *Huffington Post*, January 29, 2012.
Cris Barrish	"Crackdown on Painkiller Epidemic Hurts Legitimate Patients," *USA Today*, February 27, 2012.
Victoria Bekiempis	"America's Prescription Drug Addiction Suggests a Sick Nation," *Guardian*, April 9, 2012.
Lisa Girion, Scott Glover, and Doug Smith	"Drug Deaths Now Outnumber Traffic Fatalities in U.S., Data Show," *Los Angeles Times*, September 17, 2011.
Sanjay Gupta	"The Truth About Prescription Medication Addiction," CNN.com, February 22, 2012.
Jeffrey Kluger	"The New Drug Crisis: Addiction by Prescription," *Time*, September 13, 2010.
Andrew Kolodny	"Opioids Are Rarely the Answer," *New York Times*, February 16, 2012.
Amy Pavuk	"Rx for Danger: Oxycodone Crackdown Drives Addicts to Other Drugs," *Orlando Sentinel* (Florida), July 28, 2012.
Lloyd I. Sederer	"Prescription Drug Abuse: The New Killer on the Block," *Huffington Post*, November 8, 2011.
Jacob Sullum	"Drug Control vs. Pain Control," *Reason*, April 27, 2011.
Maia Szalavitz	"Methadone: A Major Driver of Prescription Painkiller Overdose Deaths," *Time*, July 3, 2012.

OPPOSING
VIEWPOINTS®
SERIES

CHAPTER 3

How Should Government Policies Address Prescription Drug Abuse?

Chapter Preface

Prescription drug monitoring programs (PDMPs) have been hailed by many in law enforcement and public health as an effective tool to fight the epidemic of prescription drug abuse in the United States. PDMPs allow states to collect data on drug prescriptions from pharmacies and physicians, analyze the information gathered, and provide prescription drug data to authorized law enforcement and health care officials. Physicians, pharmacists, dentists, nurse practitioners, and other authorized health professionals can access a PDMP database to review a patient's drug prescription record to determine whether patients are receiving controlled substances from other providers and to assist in the prevention of prescription drug abuse. State and local law enforcement utilize this information to identify and deter or prevent drug abuse and enforce state drug laws. Public health officials use it to support access to legitimate medical use of controlled substances, develop public health initiatives in response to use and abuse trends, and tailor educational programs that inform individuals about PDMPs and prescription drug abuse.

The first prescription drug monitoring program in the United States was developed in New York in 1918. The goal of that early program was the same as it is today: to monitor drug prescriptions throughout the state and prevent drug abuse and diversion, which is the use of prescription drugs for recreational purposes. Over the decades, several other states put similar programs in place. Information was collected through the use of duplicate prescription forms, which allowed state health departments to have a record of what was being prescribed, when it was prescribed, and to whom it was prescribed.

In the 1990s, the emergence of the Internet streamlined the installation and management of PDMPs for the states. The first electronic PDMP was established in Oklahoma in 1991. Today, thirty-seven states have operational PDMPs that have the capacity to receive and distribute controlled substance prescription information to authorized users. Eleven states have authorized PDMPs but do not have operational systems as of yet.

The case of Florida underscores the economic and political challenges of authorizing and implementing PDMPs. For years, the state has been designated the epicenter of prescription drug abuse, with many criminals buying drugs at "pill mills" (pain management clinics known for writing prescriptions for painkillers with little oversight) and then traveling across state lines to sell them illegally on the black market. Florida is also known for "doctor shopping," in which a patient goes from doctor to doctor to obtain multiple prescriptions for powerful narcotics. To combat these practices and get a handle on the prescription drug problem in the state, the Florida legislature approved the creation of a statewide PDMP database in 2009.

However, before the PDMP in Florida could become operational, a political controversy over the system erupted. In 2011 Governor Rick Scott called for repeal of the program, arguing that there was no money to implement the system. In difficult economic times, the funding for a large government program was a tough sell to many citizens. Scott eliminated the Office of Drug Control, which was working with the state Department of Health to make the database operational. He also cited concerns over privacy, contending that the database held the potential to violate the privacy of law-abiding physicians, pharmacists, and patients. Many Floridians were concerned about government intrusion into doctor-patient relationships and the personal information of consumers. Instead, Scott advocated spending the state's resources on enforcing existing policies to go after criminals exploiting the system.

Despite the tough opposition from Governor Scott and other political groups, Florida's PDMP became operational in September 2011. The controversy over PDMPs is one of the topics examined in the following chapter, which focuses on government policies to combat prescription drug abuse. Other viewpoints in the chapter explore decriminalizing drugs, drug take-back programs, and the regulation of prescription pain-killers.

> *"Approaching our drug problem through the frame of a 'war on drugs' is overly simplistic and does not adequately address what is, in reality, a very complicated public health and public safety problem."*

A Balance of Public Health and Safety Is Best to Address Prescription Drug Abuse

R. Gil Kerlikowske

R. Gil Kerlikowske is the director of the White House Office of National Drug Control Policy. In the following viewpoint, he states that recent reports that the war on drugs has become a barrier to effective pain treatment for many Americans is not true. Kerlikowske argues that US government policy is not focused on persecuting doctors for prescribing pain medications or legitimate patients suffering with chronic pain but is actually a well-considered balance of public health and safety strategies to reduce drug use and its consequences. In addition, he shows that there is little evidence to prove that pain relievers are difficult to obtain. He argues that the cause of the undertreatment of pain in the United States can be traced to a lack of knowledge on effective pain management among physicians, patients, policy makers, and insurers.

R. Gil Kerlikowske, "Setting the Record Straight: Responding to the Prescription Drug Epidemic," *Huffington Post*, March 22, 2012.

As you read, consider the following questions:

1. According to government statistics cited by Kerlikowske, how many drug-induced deaths were there in 2009?

2. How many people died from a drug overdose every day in 2007, according to government statistics cited in the viewpoint?

3. According to the Centers for Disease Control and Prevention (CDC) data cited by Kerlikowske, how much larger was the quantity of prescription pain relievers sold to pharmacies, hospitals, and doctors' offices in 2010 than in 1999?

Last week [in March 2012] I traveled to Vienna, Austria, to serve as head of the U.S. delegation to the United Nations Commission on Narcotic Drugs, the organization committed to implementing international agreements to control the abuse, production and trafficking of drugs while also ensuring their availability for medical and scientific purposes. In my remarks before the commission, I outlined the [President Barack] Obama administration's 21st-century approach to drug control policy—an approach that rejects the false choice between an enforcement-centric "war on drugs" on the one hand and the extreme notion of drug legalization on the other. After all, addiction is not a moral failing on the part of the individual—science shows that drug addiction is a disease of the brain that can be prevented and treated.

With this in mind, the Obama administration has adopted a mainstream approach to the drug problem, employing a balance of public health and safety approaches to reduce drug use and its consequences. All of these policies are grounded in science and research—not politics or ideology. I was therefore surprised when I read Radley Balko's three-part *HuffPost*, series on prescription pain relievers. The series is based on the false premise that "The biggest barrier to effective pain treatment continues to be bad public policy, much of it driven by the war on drugs."

A Comprehensive Strategy

My first act upon being appointed President Obama's drug policy advisor in 2009 was to discard the "war on drugs" approach to formulating drug policy. Approaching our drug problem through the frame of a "war on drugs" is overly simplistic and does not adequately address what is, in reality, a very complicated public health and public safety problem. All of us know someone who suffers from a substance use disorder—we are not at war with our own people. That is why today we are spending more at the federal level on drug education and treatment than on domestic law enforcement, which still serves a vital role in protecting communities from drug-related crime. It is also why we continue to lead the world in progressive evidence-based change through our central policy document—the National Drug Control Strategy—which outlines over 100 specific actions to make America healthier and safer. This balanced approach extends to our efforts to reduce prescription drug abuse, efforts that are based on the premise that we must work to prevent the abuse of prescription drugs while also ensuring legitimate access to lifesaving medications for those who need them.

There is no question prescription painkillers are essential for millions of Americans. However, we cannot lose sight of how serious our nation's prescription drug abuse problem has become and the thousands of victims it has created. According to the Centers for Disease Control and Prevention (CDC), prescription drug abuse is now an epidemic:

- National data show that by 2009, drug-induced deaths had become the number one cause of injury death in

America, with the 39,147 drug-induced deaths exceeding the number of deaths from motor vehicle crashes (36,216).

- The overall drug overdose death rate in the United States roughly tripled between 1991 and 2011, and in 2007 about 100 people in this country died per day from drug overdoses.

- In 2008 (the last year for which we have data), almost 15,000 Americans died from an unintentional drug overdose involving prescription pain relievers.

- The rate of overdose deaths involving prescription pain relievers experienced a nearly fourfold increase from 1999–2008.

- The consequences stretch far beyond just deaths. In 2008, for every one death involving prescription pain relievers, there were also eight treatment admissions for abuse, 31 emergency department visits for misuse or abuse, 125 people who abused or were dependent on prescription pain relievers and 838 people who used prescription pain relievers nonmedically during the year.

A False Premise

In his series, Mr. Balko trains a skeptical eye on this data, and yet he still reaches the unavoidable conclusion that it is "likely" more people are taking pain relievers, more people are becoming addicted and more people are dying of drug overdose. In doing so, he reluctantly concedes a fact that has been accepted by the mainstream public health and pain specialist community.

At the same time, data clearly refute Mr. Balko's claim that prescription drug abuse prevention efforts are unduly restricting the availability of opioid pain relievers for legal use. A 2006 study published in the journal *Pain Medicine* found that

National Drug Control Strategy Goals to Be Attained by 2015

Goal 1: Curtail illicit drug consumption in America

1a. Decrease the 30-day prevalence of drug use among 12- to 17-year-olds by 15 percent

1b. Decrease the lifetime prevalence of 8th graders who have used drugs, alcohol, or tobacco by 15 percent

1c. Decrease the 30-day prevalence of drug use among young adults aged 18–25 by 10 percent

1d. Reduce the number of chronic drug users by 15 percent

Goal 2: Improve the public health and public safety of the American people by reducing the consequences of drug abuse

2a. Reduce drug-induced deaths by 15 percent

2b. Reduce drug-related morbidity by 15 percent

2c. Reduce the prevalence of drugged driving by 10 percent

National Drug Control Strategy, 2012. www.whitehouse.gov.

when adequate documentation exists in the medical record, the risk of civil, criminal or administrative action being taken by the DEA [Drug Enforcement Administration] against a physician for prescribing opioids for a chronic pain patient is small. And a 2008 study published in *Pain Medicine* found that there appears to be little objective basis for concern that pain specialists have been "singled out" for prosecution or administrative sanctioning for such offences. Those health care professionals who have been prosecuted under due process of law for criminal drug violations have clearly shown a wanton disregard for patient safety. There is also little evidence to show that pain relievers are difficult to obtain. In fact, according to the CDC, the quantity of prescription pain relievers sold to pharmacies, hospitals and doctors' offices was four times larger in 2010 than in 1999. This means that enough prescription pain relievers were prescribed in 2010 to medicate every American adult with a typical dose of 5 mg [milligrams] of hydrocodone every four hours for an entire month.

Our efforts to prevent prescription drug abuse are not the cause of the undertreatment of pain in the United States. Rather, the problem results from a lack of awareness among health care professionals, patients, policy makers and insurers about the need to manage pain and how to safely and effectively do so. The final report from the American Medical Association's first National Pain Summit in 2010 found that: "The top three barriers to receiving adequate patient care were 1) workforce issues with lack of competent pain providers, 2) lack of knowledge by peers and/or patients regarding the field of pain medicine and 3) lack of public knowledge regarding pain issues."

A Top Priority

Both the undertreatment of pain and the epidemic of prescription drug abuse are issues of serious concern for the administration. Through the National Institutes of Health Pain Consortium, the federal government is working to establish "Centers of Excellence in Pain Education" at medical, dental, pharmacy and nursing schools across the nation. The centers will help to give health care professionals a solid understanding of pain as part of their basic education, improving pain treatment while also reducing the risk of prescription opioid abuse. Through the administration's prescription drug abuse prevention plan, we are working with federal, state and local agencies—and Americans across the country—to reverse the rising tide of overdose deaths and bring an end to the epidemic of prescription drug abuse. The importance of providing an effective measure of control while also allowing legitimate access is made clear on the very first page of the plan: "The potent medications science has developed have great potential for relieving suffering, as well as great potential for abuse. . . . Accordingly, any policy in this area must strike a balance between our desire to minimize abuse of prescription drugs and the need to ensure access for their legitimate use."

We can address these two problems together and, in doing so, ensure that Americans are able to get treatment for chronic pain without falling victim to the disease of addiction.

> *"Fear of addiction may be deeply in-grained, but our understanding of severe pain and its consequences remains inadequate, and much of it recent."*

Strict Regulation of Prescription Drugs Harms Patients Suffering from Chronic Pain

Elizabeth MacCallum

Elizabeth MacCallum is a reporter for Maclean's. *In the following viewpoint, she suggests that a modern-day opium war is raging over the treatment of chronic pain. According to MacCallum, with the best drugs for pain being addictive opium-based painkillers, many doctors under-prescribe pain medication for patients suffering from chronic pain over concerns that it will cause addiction. Some physicians do not want to be under investigation by law enforcement for prescribing prescription painkillers, she asserts. For example, MacCallum explains, Ontario has so strictly regulated the use of OxyContin that it is rarely prescribed by doctors. MacCallum argues that it is unethical for adults to have to suffer from chronic, debilitating pain because of a climate of fear and media scaremongering.*

As you read, consider the following questions:

1. According to Dr. Mary Lynch, as quoted by MacCallum, how many deaths from prescription painkiller overdoses are intentional suicides?

2. What percentage of North Americans does the author estimate have reported suffering from chronic pain?

3. In what year did Purdue Pharma first market OxyContin, according to the viewpoint?

"Chronic pain is even worse to live with than lung, cardiac or liver disease. Bad chronic pain is connected with the worst quality of life. People don't realize that it is a disease on its own, not just a symptom."

That's a pain warrior talking, a warrior who has been in the battle against pain for over 25 years. Dr. Mary Lynch's new patients wait more than two years to see her because of her renown as an unusually empathetic physician who understands the complexities of living with pain, day in, day out, year after year.

In 2010, she co-authored a brief to the parliamentary committee on palliative [focused on relieving pain and providing comfort vs. curing disease] and compassionate care, as did Margaret Somerville, an ethicist at McGill University, who stated a now-classic credo for pain-management workers: "People in pain have a right to fully adequate pain relief treatment. Physicians should not fear that giving adequate pain relief treatment is unethical or illegal; in fact, they should fear the ethical and legal consequences of not doing so."

Ethical? Legal? These are not concerns that should afflict a fight to ease people's suffering, yet they are. In pain treatment, there is an elephant in the room as old, if not older, than the dreaded opium dens of China's dissipated Qing Dynasty.

The Challenge of Treating Chronic Pain

The most effective drugs today for severe and chronic pain are based on opium, or chemicals with the same structure, all potentially addictive. So, on the one hand, you have pain specialists like Lynch, a past president of the Canadian Pain Society and a professor at the Queen Elizabeth II Health Sciences Centre at Dalhousie University in Halifax, on the front lines with patients in pain, who talks with fervour of "fulfilling" the United Nations Universal Declaration of Human Rights; on the other hand, you have doctors who specialize in addiction who say prescribing opioids can contravene a doctor's duty to do no harm by creating addicts. Some doctors steadfastly refuse to prescribe opioids, even when their patients are in severe pain. That, in its starkest terms, is why we now have a modern-day opium war. . . .

The War Against Opioid Painkillers

For evidence of the war, look no further than the rhetoric trumpeted in the media in the immediate aftermath of Ontario's announcement in mid-February [2012] that it would no longer pay for a leading brand of potent painkillers. As of March 1, the province delisted OxyContin and its replacement OxyNeo. Any doctor who wants to prescribe the long-acting oxycodone to new patients will now need to prove another attempt at long-acting pain treatment has failed.

Nova Scotia is following suit, limiting the drug to use for cancer-related pain and palliative care. Prince Edward Island already had strict criteria for OxyContin prescriptions and will not pay for the new, safer replacement.

The war on this drug—no other opioid is being delisted—is driven by what editorialists describe as "an epidemic of opioid addiction," fuelled by stories about pharmacy break-ins, inquests into prescription-drug deaths and tragic tales of lives undone. The focus of it all is the prevailing connection of opioids to drug addicts and accidental deaths, with little consideration for their proper need and use as painkillers.

"The popular scare comes from the deaths," says Dr. Peter Selby, clinical director of the addictions programs at the Centre for Addiction and Mental Health in Toronto. "My personal opinion about OxyContin is that it was designed to be addictive. Thirty-five per cent of the drug is immediate release for a fast effect."

Not all deaths involving OxyContin are accidental. According to Lynch, doctors who want to ban or severely restrict medical use of opioids ignore that "a significant number who died from overdoses, from 15 to 25 per cent, was not accidental but suicides because people are in such bad pain they want to kill themselves. Even with drugs, pain patients often don't get the care they need. In these drug deaths, only one side of the story is told."

A Complex and Controversial Issue

The issue is complicated and multifaceted, and hugely susceptible to easy, headline-grabbing accusations. For starters, the best drugs for pain—codeine, morphine, Demerol, ratio-Oxycocet, for example—are all addictive by nature. Before prescribing opioids, doctors are obliged to make sure their patients are not at high risk for addiction. Beyond what doctors prescribe, however, the reality is that OxyContin has replaced crack and heroin as one of the most popular street drugs. When the police manage to clean up this market, another substance will take over as the drug du jour.

Meanwhile, burglaries in pharmacies have become so frequent that many drugstores haven't been keeping OxyContin in stock, ordering it in for each prescription. Not only do pharmacists fear violent, irrational thieves, but insurance companies can charge over $10,000 a month even if a pharmacy did as little as $1,000 worth of business in opioids. And since

"Have you tried enjoying the aches and pains?" Cartoon by Roy Delgado. www.Cartoon Stock.com.

it has become an increasingly popular drug—more than 20 per cent of North Americans now report having suffered from chronic pain—there is lots left in family medicine cupboards.

"These days kids have 'pharming' parties," says Dr. Roman Jovey, medical director of CPM, Centres for Pain Management. "They throw all the pills they can find in a bowl, take a handful and down it with alcohol. They see their parents take them, so they underestimate their strength. All youth will experiment with drugs but now there is a blurring of the margins of prescription drugs and illegal street drugs."

The Fear of Addiction

Like most wars, ideology and money are key elements, and innocent citizens, particularly those disabled by pain, are the victims in the new opium wars. Jovey talks about a "societal historical fear of opioid addiction," a sort of love-hate relationship. "Addiction to opioids seems to occupy a special obsession when alcohol and smoking are even more harmful," he says.

But abuse is a particularly apt term when discussing oxycodone addiction. "When oxycodone came out, we never even thought of crushing it and snorting it or injecting it. The reason I can still sleep at night when I prescribe OxyContin is that street use is so relatively small compared with therapeutic use," says Jovey.

OxyContin

Purdue Pharma L.P. first marketed a time-release form of oxycodone called OxyContin in 1996. Its strength is that it gradually releases its painkilling medicine. The aim is to keep pain at a low level all the time, to avoid the spikes of pain requiring higher doses of fast-acting pills.

Trouble soon followed OxyContin. In 2001, West Virginia claimed Purdue Pharma violated that state's Consumer Credit [and] Protection Act, antitrust statutes, and created a public nuisance because its aggressive marketing led to "excessive, inappropriate and unnecessary prescriptions." Purdue settled three years later for US$10 million. In 2007, it paid US$19.5 million to 26 states and the District of Columbia to end their complaints. Also that year, Purdue paid more than US$600 million and pleaded guilty in federal court to resolve criminal and civil liabilities "in connection with a long-term illegal scheme to promote, market and sell OxyContin," the U.S. Food and Drug Administration announced. While Purdue Pharma Canada is associated with, but independent from, the American company, the impact has been felt here, too.

In a rare interview, pharmacologist Cornelia Hentzsch, head of Purdue Pharma Canada, explained OxyContin was actually developed "as an alternative to MS Contin, which had morphine as its main component."

Many people cannot tolerate morphine but can take other opioid drugs with fewer side effects. Feedback from doctors and patients indicated the need for a combination of fast- and slow-acting drugs in one pill. Pain-management practice accepts that a strong dose of painkiller as soon as possible reduces the amount of drug required in the long run.

"In its warnings, the publicity inadvertently gave information on how to abuse it," said Hentzsch. "We're worried we may have to take it off the market when it is such an effective pain control drug."

OxyContin in Canada

After the American scandals, Pharma's Canadian salespeople were instructed not to promote OxyContin, but rather just point out to doctors the drug's dangers and how to detect potential addicts.

"People think I'm crazy," says Hentzsch. "They see me going around doing a negative sales campaign. But I'm shocked by the lack of monitoring of patients. We're trying to increase controls through professional associations. I've been to [Health Canada's] Office of Controlled Substances asking for limitations on the numbers of high-dose tablets. We've been constantly searching. You don't solve the problem of substance abuse by removing one particular substance. It is something deeply ingrained in our society."

Ironically, the provinces have taken matters in hand, just when OxyNeo, impossible to snort, inhale or inject, makes a much safer drug available.

Treating Chronic Pain

Fear of addiction may be deeply ingrained, but our understanding of severe pain and its consequences remains inadequate, and much of it recent. Pain begins with birth for mother and child. Doctors circumcised babies with no analgesic at all, apparently thinking they didn't feel pain despite their screams. Premature babies who spent months in hospital before even coming home were put through hundreds of procedures, even excruciating ones like spinal punctures, without anaesthetics. Fortunately, pediatricians now know better, but only within the last 20 years.

Many adults still have trouble getting pain treatment—even before the delisting. One of Jovey's patients was turned down by more than 20 doctors when looking for a new general practitioner to replace a retired one. It takes patience, extra work, and even some courage to take on a patient with chronic pain: in addition to the mountains of paperwork behind prescribing opioids, and the omnipresent fear of onerous inspection by the provincial colleges of physicians and surgeons, there's just too much time required to deal with the complicated issues of chronic pain which—even on a good day—cannot be cured, only managed.

With many family doctors reluctant to deal with patients requiring long-term opioid use, the inevitable result is a small number of doctors come to be known as good "pain" doctors. Then, anti-opioid lobbyists criticize them for either overprescribing or prescribing carelessly. In fact, most pain specialists say the biggest problem in Canada for pain patients is the under-prescribing of drugs.

The Need for Opioid Painkillers

"I have a whole caseload of nerve-damaged patients. Most of them are in terrible pain and they aren't properly medicated," laments therapist Carol Moore of Toronto. She specializes in patients who have gone through severe neurological trauma, like car accidents. Most of them live reduced lives with permanent brain damage and physical handicaps, and have gone from being healthy one day, to being in a wheelchair or worse the next.

Moore is an old pro but she loses her professional veneer when the subject of pain comes up. "They're only given Tylenol 3 and they are suffering!" One of Moore's patients suffers from a neurological disorder caused by a minor, low-impact collision when she pressed back her thumb on the driver's wheel. The result has been complex regional pain syndrome; her entire arm, up to her neck, is in agony. From an ordinary healthy existence, her life has changed irrevocably. She needs to take so many opioid medications to deal with the pain that she once didn't realize a fire alarm was screaming above her head in her own room. She didn't even realize she should vacate her apartment immediately. As a result, she has had to accept 24-hour care, which costs her dearly. In addition to the medication, once a month she goes in for a nerve block, a surgical injection of steroids and anaesthetics that dulls the nerve paths in her arm. As the days of the month go by, waiting for that next stab of relief, her arm feels increasingly like it is immersed in boiling oil.

Because nerve blocks become less effective with repetition, she can't have them too frequently. Her whole life centres around her caregivers and surviving until the next nerve block, the daily pain somewhat relieved by regular long-acting opioids, and extra, fast-acting ones for even more pain than usual. At least she has doctors who understand her need for pain control and give her more than Tylenol 3. People like her don't get much mention in the media. The fact that the suicide rate of people suffering long-term chronic pain may be twice as high as the normal population isn't mentioned either.

Opioids don't get rid of chronic pain and for the most part, the medical system does not accommodate the myriad other treatments that should accompany these drugs. Nevertheless, many people find that these opioids just help them get through the day with less debilitating pain. They may be able to look after their children again, without collapsing in tears of frustration. Or they may be able to sleep through most of the night, again with the help of opioid medication, along with all the other pain-management exercises and paraphernalia.

What is clear is that the scaremongering often distorts figures and the response. It makes people in pain fear taking what can help them. It makes doctors reluctant to prescribe drugs their patients need, and it distracts attention from the real need for education in the field of pain management. The first reason people see their family doctor is because of pain. No medical school in Canada offers a specialized degree in pain management—even Dalhousie, where Mary Lynch fights on in a war where the battle lines keep changing.

> *"Shedding moral pretenses, one needs to look at the illegal drug business in America as just another capitalist racket. No better, no worse."*

Decriminalizing Drugs Would Reduce Prescription Drug Abuse

David Rosen

David Rosen is a writer and journalist. In the following viewpoint, he contends that the war on drugs has been a very expensive failure at reducing drug addiction in the United States—but has succeeded in feeding the prison-industrial complex, drug cartels, and the financial sector that make money off the illegal drug racket. Decriminalizing illegal drugs—including drugs like OxyContin and Prozac that can be legally obtained only with a doctor's prescription—would save the country billions of dollars and end the mass incarceration of millions of Americans, Rosen asserts. In recent years, Rosen maintains, there has been a trend toward more rational drug laws, including the decriminalization of marijuana and fair sentencing.

David Rosen "America's Illegal Drug Complex," *CounterPunch*, November 11–13, 2011.

As you read, consider the following questions:

1. According to Jeffrey Miron and Katherine Waldock, as quoted by Rosen, how much money would America save if it decriminalized illegal drugs?

2. How much does the author estimate the United States has spent on the war on drugs since 1982?

3. According to IMS Health estimates cited in the viewpoint, what were the prescription drug sales in the United States in 2009?

American capitalism consists of a constellation of rackets. The Occupy Wall Street movement has focused a spotlight on the banking and financial services racket. Others have exposed the military-industrial complex, the extraction industries, the insurance, pharmaceutical and health care system, the agriculture and food combine and the communications trust.

Each racket is distinguished by the self-serving, intimate interrelation of private corporate interests and the public government, whether at the federal, state or local level. Each racket consist of a host of distinct business elements, organized through both vertical and horizontal operations, no matter whether the business is conducted "legally" or not. Each is charged with maximizing profit.

Rackets succeed by enabling private corporations to exploit the power and wealth of the public trough, the state. Rackets do this in different ways, combining direct contracts, subsidies and tax breaks that further engorge the corporate bottom line.

Three Types of US Rackets

One racket involves direct federal contracts to private companies, often with cost-plus agreements; in 2010, an estimated $180 billion went to the top 20 contractors. This is the model of the military-industrial complex.

A second racket is characterized by the transfer or "externalization" of the social costs associated with a company's product to consumers and taxpayers. This is most evident in the role of government subsidies and tax breaks associated with the (indirect) health-related costs that underwrite the extraction (e.g., air & water pollution) and food (e.g., obesity) industries.

A third type of racket involves the use of the legal system to maximize private gain and exemplified by the prison-industrial complex. The criminalization of "illegal" drug taking as an unacceptable practice, like alcohol during Prohibition, has enabled many third parties, including government agencies, banks and private contractors, to profit from other people's suffering.

Shedding moral pretenses, one needs to look at the illegal drug business in America as just another capitalist racket. No better, no worse. The street dope dealer is just another version of the day stock trader, the only difference is their legal status, although their social status, clothing and marketing message might be the same.

The War on Drugs

Pres. Richard Nixon declared war on illegal drugs in 1971; Nancy Reagan launched her fateful "War on Drugs" campaign in 1982; and Pres. Ronald Reagan signed the National Security [Decision] Directive 221 in 1986 that transformed the drug war into a major, national conflict.

A recent article laid out the topography of America's "drug" culture. In it, the line between the legal and the illegal, like that between the moral and immoral or the licit and illicit, is acknowledged as a terrain of social conflict, one that changes over time through popular struggle and social conditions. This characterized the 1920s, the era of alcohol prohibition; we are amidst such a period today.

While it is impossible to tabulate the full costs of U.S. drug use, even the most conservative estimates are staggering. Millions of Americans (some estimates run as high as 20% of the population, 60 million people) either regularly abuse or are addicted to "drugs," whether "legal" (i.e., prescription) or illegal (e.g., marijuana, cocaine, etc.), whether a commercial or underground product. And this does not include alcohol, a legal intoxicant. America is a drugged-out nation.

One estimate places the costs associated with drug addiction/abuse in the U.S. at "over $484 billion per year." This includes the costs for policing, health care, crime and lost earnings. Two academic experts, Jeffrey Miron and Katherine Waldock, estimate that decriminalizing (i.e., regulating and taxing) currently illegal drugs would save Americans approximately $41 billion a year in federal and state government expenditures relating to drug enforcement.

The Prison-Industrial Complex

According to the Global Commission on Drug Policy, "Drug Policy and the incarceration of low-level drug offenders is the primary cause of mass incarceration in the United States." The U.S. has the largest prison population on the planet with more than 2.3 million people currently incarcerated; between 1987 and 2007, the federal prisoner population nearly tripled from nearly 600,000 to 1.6 million. Currently, one out of 100 adults is in jail or prison and one out of 31 adults is in jail, in prison, on probation or on parole. The report points outs that 40 percent of drug arrests are for simple possession of marijuana.

Going further, the commission estimates that, in 2006, the federal and state governments spent $68 billion on incarceration, up from a meager $6.9 billion in 1980. During the ten-year period between 1985 and 1995, new prisons opened at a pace of one facility a week.

According to a recent ACLU [American Civil Liberties Union] report, "Banking on Bondage: Private Prisons and Mass Incarceration," for-profit companies are responsible for approximately 6 percent of state prisoners and 16 percent of federal prisoners. It points out "in 2010, the two largest private prison companies alone received nearly $3 billion in revenue, and their top executives, according to one source, each received annual compensation packages worth well over $3 million." The war-on-drugs racket has turned out to be very profitable for some.

Since Nancy Reagan's campaign, Americans have spent an estimated $1 trillion in this losing war. It's been a war in which the battle has only gotten worse over time. In 2010, the Associated Press acknowledged the following cautionary concern: "This year, 25 million Americans will snort, swallow, inject and smoke illicit drugs, about 10 million more than in 1970, with the bulk of those drugs imported from Mexico."

The Consumers and the Marketplace

In line with the business model of many American industrial rackets, the illegal drug racket depends on the tribute collected at its retail outlets. These commercial transactions are conducted anywhere and everywhere, be it on a deserted street corner or at a local store, at a dealer's apartment or the customer's home.

Like the legal alcohol consumer, the illegal-drug customer base can be divided between "hard core" and "casual" users. Teresa Novellino, writing on Portfolio.com, estimates the casual base at 13 million people, including Americans who "think nothing about occasionally buying a gram of cocaine, a few hits of ecstasy or a quarter ounce of weed to party with their friends on the weekends." She estimates the hard-core user base, those having "more serious drug habits, and may spend $100–$500 dollars a week on purchasing their drugs," at between 5 and 6 million. Referring to U.S. government data (which she does not specify), Novellino estimates that "these two groups—hard-core users and casual users—spend approximately $60 billion dollars a year."

In addition to old-fashioned illegal drug dealing, a new "legal" drug industry now flourishes. According to Ethan Nadelmann of the Drug Policy Alliance, medical marijuana is legal in 16 states and the District of Columbia. In addition, more than 1,000 medical marijuana "dispensaries" operate throughout the country; efforts are under way in Arizona, Maine, New York and Rhode Island to set up similar clinics. . . .

Nevertheless, "legal" marijuana sales are becoming a viable specialty business. In seven of the nine territories where "clinics" operate (excluding DC and NJ), an estimated 730,000 people have "shopped" at one of these dispensaries. In California, for example, medical marijuana clinics generate an estimated $1.3 billion in sales and $105 million in taxes. For tax-hungry state and local governments, a marijuana dollar is no different than revenue garnered from any other sales transaction.

Illegal Prescription Drugs

In late September [2011], federal agents arrested 37 people for operating an illegal prescription-drug ring at a Boeing Co. plant in Ridley Park, PA, where the Chinook military helicopter is manufactured. Of those charged, 23 were indicted for distributing drugs including Actiq, OxyContin and Xanax.

IMS Health, a pharmaceutical industry research firm, estimated that in 2009 prescription drug sales in the U.S. topped $300 billion. The U.S. Department of Health and Human Services' Substance Abuse and Mental Health Services Administration (SAMHSA) found abuse of prescription painkillers increased 400 percent between 1998 and 2008. The abuse of prescription medications ranks second to marijuana in terms of frequency of illegal drug use.

The Centers for Disease Control [and Prevention] notes that over the last 10 years the percentage of Americans who took at least one prescription drug in the past month increased to 48 percent from 44 percent; the use of two or more drugs increased to 31 percent from 25 percent; and the use of five or more drugs nearly doubled to 11 percent from 6 percent. In 2007–2008, 1 out of every 5 children and 9 out of 10 older Americans reported using at least one prescription drug in the past month.

Scarier still, the Florida Medical Examiners Commission found that the abuse of prescription drugs has outstripped illegal drugs as a cause of death. In 2007, three times as many people died taking a legal drug than by cocaine, heroin and all methamphetamines put together. "The abuse [of pharmaceutical drugs] has reached epidemic proportions," said Lisa McElhaney, a sergeant in the Broward County Sheriff's Office. "It's just explosive."

Crossing the line to conventional "illegal" drugs, traditional business rules of production and distribution operate but with a different cost-of-goods model. According to an analysis by Abt Associates, "What America's Users Spend on Illegal Drugs," "like any commodities business the closer you are to the source the cheaper the product." It estimates that processed cocaine in Colombia sells for $1,500 per kilo and is sold in the U.S. for as much as $66,000 a kilo. A similar pattern is in effect for heroin; a kilo in Pakistan costs $2,600 but retails for $130,000 in the U.S.

And a homegrown synthetic drug like methamphetamine, which costs between $300 to $500 per kilo to produce, has a retail street price of up to $60,000 per kilo. CNN Money estimates the street vs. retail price for a single tablet of some commonly trafficked drugs as follows: Oxycontin: $50 to $80 on the street vs. $6 when sold legally; Oxycodone: $12 to $40 on the street vs. $6 retail; Percocet: $10 to $15 vs. $6 retail; and Vicodin: $5 to $25 vs. $1.50 retail.

Who Is Profiting?

Since Pres. Nixon launched the war against "illegal" drugs in 1971, politicians, police departments, think tanks and innumerable private corporations have shared in the multibillion-dollar antidrug gravy racket.

Those who have paid the harshest penalties in this war are those imprisoned in the government's round-'em-up and three-strikes campaigns. Between 1980 and 2006, the number of people incarcerated for drug offenses in state and federal prisons increased 1,412 percent to 361,276 from 23,900; today, the drug-related prison population is estimated at around 500,000. Most of those arrested are nonviolent offenders. In 2010, approximately $40 billion in taxpayer dollars were spent in fighting the war on drugs.

Making matters worse, there is little evidence that imprisonment or harsh sentences has had any noticeable effect on the drug trade. Drug sales have not significantly fallen; drug use has not declined; public safety has not improved. Mexico, the great supplier of drugs to the U.S., is a nation at war— and the war spills over with dreadful consequences.

The only winners in the war on drugs have been the drug cartels, the prison-industrial complex and the U.S. banks and other middlemen who facilitate the "washing" of illegal drug money.

The Role of the Financial Sector

The profiteering by the financial sector in the drug trade often goes overlooked. Antonio Maria Costa, head of the UN [United Nations] Office on Drugs and Crime, argued in 2009 that the proceeds of the illegal drug trade were "the only liquid investment capital" available to some banks on the brink of collapse during the fiscal crisis of 2007–2009 period. He estimated that a majority of the $352 billion (£216 billion) of drugs profits was absorbed into the economic system as a result.

In March 2010, Wachovia (which had been absorbed by Wells Fargo in December 2008) copped a plea for laundering some $378.4 billion from Mexican-currency-exchange houses from 2004 to 2007. "Wachovia's blatant disregard for our banking laws gave international cocaine cartels a virtual carte blanche to finance their operations," said Jeffrey Sloman, the federal prosecutor of the case. (Sloman did not provide an estimate of the bank's fees generated from its illegal practices.)

In keeping with the federal government policy of coddling the nation's biggest banks, the Wachovia/BofA [Bank of America] fine was for $160 million, less than 2 percent of the bank's 2009 profits of $12.3 billion; also in 2009, Well Fargo secured a federal bailout of $25 billion. Crime pays.

Other U.S. banks that have been implicated in questionable money laundering schemes include Israel Discount Bank of New York, Harris Bank in Chicago and JPMorgan Chase.

The Need for a More Rational Drug Policy

In the face of the mounting recession, both the federal and state governments are being forced to cut back on the staggering amounts of money doled out in the failed war on drugs. In California, New York and a dozen other states, nonviolent offenders, most often those arrested for illegal drug possession, are being pushed out of the prison door in an effort to save money. In New York, for example, prison closings are projected to save the state $184 million over the next two years.

Equally revealing, in 2010, after nearly two decades of enforcement of the Anti-Drug Abuse Acts of 1986 and 1988, which established excessive mandatory penalties for crack cocaine, Congress passed and President [Barack] Obama signed the Fair Sentencing Act that normalized mandatory minimum sentences for crack and powdered cocaine. Federal officials still enforce anti-marijuana polices with occasional raids on "clinics."

A somewhat more rational drug policy may be taking shape as evident in efforts to decriminalize "medical" marijuana, to adjust crack penalties and to remove from prison those incarcerated for nonviolent drug crimes. The fact that "public" monies are too tight to keep funding the failed "war on drugs" has forced policy makers to acknowledge that forced prohibition does not work—something the public has known for a long time.

The Failure of the War on Drugs

Four decades ago, Nixon launched America's modern prohibition movement, this one out to ban all non-alcohol intoxicants. Nixon's policies have been continued (and, in many ways, made harsher) by all subsequent presidents. They are a failure.

A new, rational and radical approach to "illegal" drugs is in order. What most "experts" seem to acknowledge but can't say is simple: like with rationalization of the alcohol industry that followed the ending of Prohibition, the illegal drug "business" needs to be rationalized. In this way, drugs production would be regulated, sales taxed and its "abusers" (i.e., addicts) seen as patients as opposed to criminals.

> *"In the 1980s and '90s, the U.S. beat back the cocaine and heroin epidemics, not by legalization or decriminalization, but by tough law enforcement, strong prevention and education programs and public outcry."*

Decriminalizing Drugs Would Not Prevent Prescription Drug Abuse

William J. Bennett

William J. Bennett is an author, a CNN contributor, and a former director of the Office of National Drug Control Policy. In the following viewpoint, Bennett argues that the recent movement to legalize drugs is misguided, because legalization would not prevent the misuse and abuse of drugs. In fact, he asserts, it would accelerate it and result in more deaths. Bennett points out that in places where drugs have been decriminalized, particularly the Netherlands and Portugal, there have been significant problems. He suggests that the United States needs a national campaign to fight drug abuse.

As you read, consider the following questions:

1. According to Arianna Huffington as quoted by Bennett, how much is the United States spending a year on the war on drugs?

2. How many Americans died from prescription drug overdoses in 2007, according to the Office of National Drug Control Policy as cited by Bennett?

3. Why does Bennett say that the Netherlands is going to ban foreigners from the country's pot shops in 2013?

On the evening of Whitney Houston's death, renowned recording artist Tony Bennett told the audience of Clive Davis' Beverly Hills party, "First it was Michael Jackson, then it was Amy Winehouse, and now, the magnificent Whitney Houston. I'd like to have every gentleman and lady in this room commit themselves to get our government to legalize drugs—so they'll have to get it through a doctor, not to some gangsters who just sell it under the table."

Bennett's idiotic comments were followed closely by the often original, but in this case mistaken, Arianna Huffington.

On Monday morning's edition of *CNN Starting Point with Soledad O'Brien*, she agreed with Bennett: "The point I think is absolutely fair—that the war on drugs has failed, and we are not acknowledging it. We are spending over $50 billion a year fighting a war that has become a war on our own people."

Legalizing Drugs Would Not Have Saved Whitney Houston

First, we do not know the immediate cause of Houston's death. But we do know that she had a long and public struggle with drugs, both legal and illegal. But legalizing drugs and making them more readily available would not have saved her life, or the life of Michael Jackson, or the thousands of other drug-related deaths each year.

Lest Tony Bennett forget, Michael Jackson died from acute propofol intoxication administered to him by a doctor.

Amy Winehouse died from alcohol poisoning—a legal, easily available substance.

A fatal combination of painkillers, sleeping pills and anti-depressants—all legal prescription drugs—killed Heath Ledger.

Brittany Murphy died from multiple drug intoxications (only prescription and over-the-counter medications according to the medical exam) combined with pneumonia.

And Anna Nicole Smith overdosed on prescription and over-the-counter drugs.

All these drugs are legal and prescribed by doctors. Contrary to what Tony Bennett and other legalizers would like to think, legalization does not prevent the abuse and misuse of drugs. In fact, it accelerates it.

The Devastating Impact of Drug Abuse

According to the Office of National Drug Control Policy, prescription drug abuse is the nation's fastest-growing drug problem. In 2007, there were 28,000 deaths from prescription drug overdoses. This is five times higher than the number in 1990. More people die in America every year from prescription drug abuse (i.e., legal and available drugs) than from heroin and cocaine combined.

The Centers for Disease Control and Prevention reported that the number of deaths from prescription narcotics increased fourfold over the past 10 years. This coincided with a fourfold increase in the number of prescriptions written for powerful painkillers. Legalization increases supply and when you increase supply, you increase the use and misuse of deadly drugs.

Drug Legalization Has Not Been Successful

As for Bennett's envy of Amsterdam, he should realize that its legalization experiment has backfired. With the legalization of marijuana came an increase in drug addictions and dependency followed by illegal drug trafficking, human trafficking and crime. After a rapid influx of organized crime, the Netherlands has announced that it will ban foreigners from the country's pot shops starting in 2013.

Drug decriminalization in Portugal has also been a failure.

As of 2007, Portugal was still the country with the most cases of injected drug-related AIDS, and it was the only European country to show a significant increase in homicides from 2001 to 2006.

"With 219 deaths by drug 'overdose' a year, Portugal has one of the worst records, reporting more than one death every two days. Along with Greece, Austria and Finland, Portugal is one of the countries that recorded an increase in drug overdose by over 30% in 2005," according to the European Monitoring Centre for Drugs and Drug Addiction.

Legalizing Drugs = More Deaths

Bennett and Huffington's misguided solutions would result in more tragic deaths like Houston's. Illicit drugs are not harmful because they are illegal, they are illegal precisely because they are harmful. It is my hope that in the national dialogue surrounding Houston's death, our country's loudest voices would speak honestly and seriously about the drug problems in America.

In the 1980s and '90s, the U.S. beat back the cocaine and heroin epidemics, not by legalization or decriminalization, but by tough law enforcement, strong prevention and education programs and public outcry. You could hardly watch TV without seeing the Partnership for a Drug-Free America's famous "This is your brain on drugs" advertisements. If we are to be successful today, we must reignite that same national effort.

Whitney Houston's mother, Cissy Houston, understood the seriousness of drug abuse. In a 2009 interview with Oprah

Winfrey, Houston recalled how her mother showed up one day at her doorstep with sheriff's officers and a court order in a drug intervention.

"(My mother) says, 'I have a court (injunction) here,'" Houston said. "Either you do it my way, or we're just not going to do this at all. We are both going to go on TV, and you're going to retire.'"

If more Americans, celebrities in particular, spoke and acted like Cissy Houston, rather than like Bennett or Huffington, fewer Americans would be victims to drug addiction.

> "With criticism mounting from con-
> sumer groups and pressure focused on
> reducing health care costs, there is a
> new sense among legislators that the
> time might finally be right for limiting
> DTC [direct-to-consumer] drug adver-
> tising."

Prescription Drug Ads Should Be Better Regulated

Naomi Freundlich

Naomi Freundlich is a journalist and blogger. In the following viewpoint, she explores the success of direct-to-consumer (DTC) advertising for pharmaceutical companies marketing drugs to the American public. She reports that there has been a recent move to more strictly regulate these ads by banning DTC advertising for new medications or providing more educational information about the drug and its effects. Freundlich finds that the Food and Drug Administration is underfunded and lacks the resources to enforce many of the regulations that are already in place concerning drug advertising. Also, she concludes, big pharmaceutical companies must do a better job with self-regulation and make a commitment to helping Americans make informed choices.

As you read, consider the following questions:

1. According to Nielsen Media Research cited in the viewpoint, how much did drug companies spend on consumer drug ads in 2008?

2. What percentage of physicians believe DTC advertising is a positive trend in health care, according to Freundlich?

3. What does Freundlich report will be in the bottom part of the proposed fact boxes for drug ads?

The pharmaceutical industry has been settling into its "good guy" role in recent days; first committing to $80 billion in cost savings over ten years to help defray the cost of health reform and then forking over $150 million to finance an ad campaign championing the administration's plan. (Of course there was that slight fall from grace when it looked as if, in exchange, PhRMA [the Pharmaceutical Research and Manufacturers of America, which represents the biopharmaceutical industry] had secured guarantees that Medicare would not be able to negotiate drug prices. . . .)

But what else can the industry do to help burnish its image with the American people? How about finally consenting to some commonsense limits on the barrage of prescription drug ads confronting consumers every time they turn on the TV or open a magazine? While a complete ban is probably not possible (in part because such a ban might violate the First Amendment) how about making prescription drug ads a lot more educational and a lot less like a hard sell for a new BMW?

Ads Hike Spending on Drugs

Direct-to-consumer advertising (DTCA) has been a boon for drug companies ever since Congress passed the Prescription Drug Marketing Act in 1987. Spending on consumer drug ads reached $5.0 billion last year [2008], according to Nielsen Media Research and Americans see up to 16 hours of drug advertising on television each year. These slick appeals for sleep aids, impotence drugs and a host of other remedies, clearly pay off. Studies show that every dollar spent on DTC ads generates four dollars in additional sales of new drugs that are often only marginally better than far cheaper, generic versions or older drugs.

Proponents of direct-to-consumer drug ads—mostly representatives from pharmaceutical companies—claim that these appeals have an educational function, bringing ill patients into their doctors' offices to receive sorely needed therapy. This benefit can be real when the advertised condition is serious and undertreated—hypertension, for example—and the treatment is highly effective and safe relative to its alternatives. But when was the last time you saw an ad on TV for a hypertension or cancer drug? Instead, aggressive advertising is much more common for therapies directed against so-called "lifestyle" problems like thin eyelashes, insomnia, toenail fungus and erectile dysfunction. And their side effects can be quite serious.

Studies have shown that direct-to-consumer advertising has fundamentally changed the way doctors and patients communicate, mostly for the worst. Fewer than 10% of physicians believe direct-to-consumer advertising (DTCA) is a positive trend in health care. Doctors report that they now spend more time explaining to patients why an expensive new drug is no better than the one they already take, or that the patient isn't suffering from a nebulous condition like fibromyalgia, just the normal aches and pains of aging.

Physicians feel pressured by patients who come in asking for these newer, more expensive (but not necessarily, better) medications by name. In a recent survey conducted by *Consumer Reports*, one-fifth of the respondents said they had asked their doctor to prescribe a drug they saw advertised on television or elsewhere: Some 70% of physicians complied with this request.

Proposed Legislation

With criticism mounting from consumer groups and pressure focused on reducing health care costs, there is a new sense among legislators that the time might finally be right for limiting DTC drug advertising. Three bills have been proposed so far, including:

1. Families for ED Advertising Decency Act—sponsored by Representative James P. Moran, (D-VA)—this House bill would give the FCC [Federal Communications Commission] power to ban ads for prescription sexual aids like Viagra and Cialis from prime-time television, on decency grounds.

2. Henry Waxman (D-CA), chair of the House Energy and Commerce Committee, supports a moratorium on DTCA for two or three years after a new drug is introduced. This action, also supported by the Institute of Medicine and the American Medical Association is necessary to prevent wide-scale advertising to the public of drugs—like Vioxx—whose long-term health effects are still unknown. Two-thirds of the drugs that are withdrawn from the market due to safety concerns have been on that market for less than three years.

3. Say No to Drug Ads—Introduced by Rep. Jerrold Nadler (D-NY), this legislation would amend the tax code so that drug companies could no longer deduct DTCA spending as a business expense.

Opposition—Not Just the Drug Companies

Opponents of limiting DTC ads argue that moratoriums on pharmaceutical advertising would violate the First Amendment protection for commercial speech. Avoiding that battle is probably a good idea, because drug industry lobbyists aren't the only ones making that argument. Drug companies are second only to the automotive industry in the amount they spend on consumer-directed advertising and in 2007, lobbyists representing media and ad agencies helped defeat Congress's attempts to further regulate DTC ads. With ad pages down throughout the industry and networks vying for sponsors, the First Amendment arguments will only get stronger.

So, barring a ban on DTC drug ads, the best way to rein in misleading and manipulative marketing is to pass regulations that tightly control how these ads are structured. The FDA [Food and Drug Administration] is supposed to be doing this already, by preventing the industry from making false and misleading claims. But when total funding for all of the FDA's programs—including enforcement—is less than half of what Big Pharma spends on direct-to-consumer advertising, it's clear that the agency just doesn't have the resources to carry out this role. With more and more pharmaceutical advertising taking place on the Internet—where, for example, it can be very difficult to discern drug company–sponsored sites from legitimate, disease advocacy sites—the FDA's ability to regulate this field has become exponentially more difficult.

Opponents of further regulation also like to point out that the industry polices itself. In 2005, PhRMA president and CEO Billy Tauzin announced that the industry group had adopted "Guiding Principles" that would promote patient education in DTC drug marketing and "foster responsible communications between patients and health care professionals to help patients achieve better health." According to Tauzin:

> "With these principles, we commit ourselves to improving the inherent educational value of advertisements. Patients need accurate and timely information and should be encouraged to discuss diseases and treatment options with their physicians."

Rebutting the Industry's Arguments

But in an editorial in the *Annals of Family Medicine*, editor and physician Kurt C. Stange, says that FDA oversight and industry self-monitoring are not working. Neither approach has stopped drug companies from promoting drugs over healthy behaviors, or has lessened the deleterious effects the ads have on doctor-patient communication.

"How are communication and health fostered by manipulating patient-clinician communication toward drugs and away from healthy behavior, or by denigrating clinician recommendations for non-pharmacological health interventions? How does a broad-based medium designed to sell to the masses promote drugs in the individualized way that is essential for safety if the message largely reaches people who are not candidates for the drug? How does it improve public health to bombard the public with the message that life is happier, more fulfilling, more socially acceptable on drugs? What are the unintended consequences of the plethora of images and messages about health that are intended to increase patient demand for drugs?"

I have further questions for the industry: If the aim of these appeals is to be educational, then why do drug companies hire multinational advertising agencies to design their ads, and not public health educators? Why are there no comparisons of therapies, clear information about risks vs. benefits and links to unbiased medical information? The answer is that today's slick direct-to-consumer ads are really not designed to be educational; they are designed to boost drug sales and profits.

The Best Solution

So what's to be done? First of all, Congress should consider Waxman's proposal for a moratorium on DTC advertising on drugs that haven't been on the market for at least two years. It shouldn't be that much of a hardship for companies—only about 15% of DTC ads are currently for drugs that are less than a year old. Limiting drug ads in this way could also help companies avoid Vioxx-like situations where widely advertised

The Impact of Direct-to-Consumer Advertising

When it comes to advertising prescription drugs on radio and television and in magazines, doctors say that, for the most part, the ads have both positive and negative effects on their patients and practices. Results of a Food and Drug Administration [FDA] survey, released in 2004, also indicate that most physicians view direct-to-consumer (DTC) ads as one of many factors that affect their medical practices and their interactions with patients.

For decades, prescription drug makers promoted their products exclusively to health care professionals, who were expected to interpret drug information for their patients. Beginning in the early 1990s, some drug manufacturers began targeting consumers due, in part, to the aging baby boomers and to an increase in the number of patients participating in their own health care decisions. Since then, DTC advertising has become a popular promotional tool. The FDA oversees the advertising of prescription drug products under the Federal Food, Drug, and Cosmetic Act and related regulations. That means the agency must ensure that prescription drug information provided by drug firms is truthful, balanced, and accurately communicated. This is accomplished through a comprehensive surveillance, enforcement, and education program, and by fostering better communication of labeling and promotional information to both health professionals and consumers.

"The Impact of Direct-to-Consumer Advertising,"
US Food and Drug Administration, August 19, 2011.
www.fda.gov.

and prescribed new drugs are found to have serious side effects only after FDA approval.

In congressional hearings on DTC ads that took place last June, representatives from Merck, Pfizer, Johnson & Johnson and Schering-Plough told legislators that they already have a voluntary 6-month moratorium on advertising for new drugs. In reality, the companies need this delay in order to get their army of drug reps out to sell doctors on the new drug before they are faced with patient requests for information.

Senators Bart Stupak and John Dingell told the companies that this wasn't long enough—they want to see a two-year moratorium on drug ads. Waxman agrees, although he now says that he is open to reserving the moratorium to drugs that are the most risky. He told *Time* magazine in February: "It doesn't have to be a full two years," Waxman says. "It's allowed to be limited to drugs that the FDA thinks might be a safety problem."

An Emphasis on Educational Aspects

Besides the moratorium, it is essential that drug advertising be educational and not just play to consumer emotions. Because, seriously, prescription drugs are not BMWs. Most people are able to think critically about car ads: they recognize that with images of beautiful women, long winding roads and a background of jazzy music, they are being sold a dream of luxury and social status. They also understand that they had better check out some price and performance comparisons before trading in the 10-year-old Escort.

By contrast, when the average person sees a television ad for Lipitor, for example (which had over $12 billion in sales in 2008) they hear "high cholesterol," "reduces risk of heart attack by 36%," and get about 45 seconds of an attractive actor talking about the drug's benefits; some 15 seconds are a rushed litany of potential risks. The viewer also knows that the FDA approved Lipitor and he believes the agency also approved the ad—there is a level of authority and trust in these ads that is not implicit in car or beer ads.

But there is a lot about statins [a class of drugs used to lower cholesterol] like Lipitor that isn't mentioned in these 60-second spots. In "Do Cholesterol Drugs Do Any Good?" John Carey of *BusinessWeek* says that Lipitor's benefits to people without significant heart disease are far less clear when the numbers are expressed this way:

> "[F]or every 100 people in the trial, which lasted 3 1/3 years, three people on placebos and two people on Lipitor had heart attacks. The difference credited to the drug? One fewer heart attack per 100 people. So to spare one person a heart attack, 100 people had to take Lipitor for more than three years. The other 99 got no measurable benefit."

In fact, Carey writes, some of those other 99 might actually have been harmed by taking Lipitor for so long—experiencing side effects that include muscle pain and cognitive problems.

Fact Boxes

One of the most promising ideas for improving the educational value of drug ads is to have them include simple-to-read "fact boxes," developed by researchers at Dartmouth's Institute for Health Policy and Clinical Practice, that are similar to the nutritional information found on most packaged food. These boxes contain two sections: the top section lists what conditions the drug can treat and who should take the medication. The bottom describes the effectiveness of the drug—and how it compares with other treatments—as well as the percentage of patients who experience different side effects.

A study by the Dartmouth researchers (which is available in the *Annals of Internal Medicine*) looked at whether adding a drug fact box to DTC ads for prescription heartburn drugs helped consumers make better choices about medication.

Some participants were given standard versions of ads for two heartburn drugs (with a long, fine-print text of drug information on the back) and others received the two ads with fact boxes replacing the fine print. In the end, some 68% of participants who got the drug fact boxes correctly identified the more effective drug; only 31% of those who got the fine print were able to discern the superior treatment.

After meeting with the Dartmouth researchers in February, the FDA's risk communication advisory committee unanimously urged the agency to require that drug fact boxes appear on all medication labels. They also recommended that they appear along with other drug information on the FDA's website. Steven Woloshin, one of the Dartmouth researchers, says that he would like to see the fact boxes replace the fine print in DTC ads as well, but the FDA doesn't have the authority to require this—that can only come from legislation.

As the nation continues to struggle with health reform, deciding what to do about direct-to-consumer drug advertising might be pushed to a back burner. But that would be a mistake. We are just one of two countries (New Zealand is the other) that allows televised hawking of drugs; it's probably not a coincidence that we also spend more than any other country on health care. These ads lead to overuse of expensive but not necessarily better drugs. They lead to the medicalization of health conditions that would be better treated with health and lifestyle changes. It's time to require a lot more integrity from Big Pharma. It's time to insist that they shift from the hard sell to helping us make informed choices about our health.

*"Across America, drug takeback pro-
grams have become increasingly popular as policy makers struggle to provide
individuals with a secure and convenient way to dispose of unused medications."*

Drug Take-Back Programs Can Limit Access to Prescription Medications

Carnevale Associates

*Carnevale Associates is a strategic planning and communications
firm. In the following viewpoint, the author finds that drug take-
back programs hold a lot of potential to limit access to prescription medications but such programs are largely untested and un-
examined. Much more research is needed to determine what
programs are the most successful and cost-effective. It is probable, the author concludes, that drug take-back programs can be
a central part of any substance abuse prevention strategy once
such programs have been fully researched and the costs calcu-
lated.*

As you read, consider the following questions:

1. According to the Substance Abuse and Mental Health Services Administration data cited in the viewpoint, how many Americans used prescription drugs nonmedically in the past month?

2. According to the 2010 National Survey on Drug Use and Health (NSDUH) cited by the author, what percentage of prescription drug users obtained drugs free from a friend or relative?

3. What percentage of the domestic take-back programs studied by Carnevale Associates collected data on both costs and medications received?

Now recognized as an epidemic and identified in President [Barack] Obama's 2011 National Drug Control Strategy as "America's fastest-growing drug problem," nonmedical use of prescription drugs outpaces all other illegal drug use except marijuana. To combat the growing nonmedical use of prescription drugs, the Office of National Drug Control Policy (ONDCP) released a Prescription Drug Abuse Prevention Plan, outlining a four-pronged effort of (1) education, (2) monitoring, (3) proper medication disposal, and (4) enforcement. Across America, drug takeback programs have become increasingly popular as policy makers struggle to provide individuals with a secure and convenient way to dispose of unused medications. Though takeback programs differ considerably, all takebacks accept some types of unused medication. To learn more about takeback programs, Carnevale Associates, LLC surveyed a number of programs to better understand their design, costs, and efficacy to support national efforts to reduce the size and scope of the prescription drug epidemic. Our analysis found that these programs vary substantially in cost and approach. In addition, we found no evidence that takeback programs affect prescription drug abuse. We conclude that additional research is needed before incorporating takebacks into any substance abuse prevention plan.

Prescription Drugs: The New Epidemic

Nonmedical use of prescription drugs is now at record levels and shows no signs of slowing. Growing numbers of first-time users (initiates) point to a continuing trend of increased use. According to the Substance Abuse and Mental Health [Services] Administration's (SAMHSA) 2010 National Survey on Drug Use and Health (NSDUH), 7 million Americans used prescription drugs nonmedically in the past month (current use). In addition, 16 million Americans used a prescription drug nonmedically at least once in 2010, up 8 percent since 2002 (14.8 million). In fact, every year since 2002, 2.4 to 2.8 million Americans have used prescription drugs nonmedically for the first time, with prescription pain relievers now attracting new users at a rate outpacing all drugs but marijuana.

Importantly, the NSDUH shows that over half of the individuals who used prescription drugs nonmedically in the past year obtained their drugs free from a friend or relative. Examining detailed data on prescription pain relievers (which constitute the majority of nonmedical use), 55 percent of users obtained drugs free from a friend/relative, 11.4 percent bought them from a friend/relative, and 4.8 percent took them from a friend/relative without asking. In total, 71 percent cited friends/relatives as the immediate source of their drug supply; however, nearly 94 percent of those individuals reported that their friends/relatives were willing partners in the diversion.

Takeback Programs: Overview

Because most nonmedical prescription drug users obtain their drugs from friends/relatives, substance abuse prevention efforts have increasingly targeted the family medicine cabinets—attempting to cut off supply by offering a safe and secure method for drug disposal. In light of their growing popularity, Carnevale Associates conducted a survey of takeback programs, examining data from 148 programs spanning 21 states and several countries. Our analysis found that takebacks vary considerably. While all takebacks accept some types of unused medication, takeback programs often have different goals, structure, and scope. Based on our findings, programs vary across five interrelated elements: (1) frequency, (2) collection mechanism, (3) drugs accepted, (4) collecting entity, and (5) geographic scope.

Frequency: Takebacks can be classified as either "event based" or "ongoing." Event-based programs offer sporadic prescheduled collections on fixed dates. The most notable example of these is the Drug Enforcement Administration (DEA) takeback days. In contrast, ongoing programs offer some form of continuous medication collection, featuring either fixed drop-off locations (e.g., pharmacies or police stations) or an option to mail back unused drugs.

Collection Mechanism: Takebacks can be classified as either "bin based," "mailback," or "person facilitated." Bin-based collections utilize specially designed locking containers into which individuals directly deposit unused drugs, mailback collections utilize USPS [United States Postal Service]-based return envelopes, and person-facilitated collections direct participants to transfer drugs directly to designated takeback personnel (predominantly at event-based collections).

Drugs Accepted: Only some takebacks accept controlled medications—the drugs targeted by substance abuse prevention programs. Under current law, only law enforcement may accept controlled substances. As a result, only takebacks located at law enforcement facilities or working with law enforcement entities may accept controlled drugs. Nearly all takebacks accept nonprescription medication (e.g., Tylenol or vitamins) in addition to uncontrolled prescription medication (e.g., antibiotics).

FDA Guidelines for Drug Disposal

- Follow any specific disposal instructions on the drug label or patient information that accompanies the medication. . . .

- Take advantage of community drug take-back programs that allow the public to bring unused drugs to a central location for proper disposal. . . . The Drug Enforcement Administration, working with state and local law enforcement agencies, is sponsoring National Prescription Drug Take-Back Days throughout the United States.

- If no instructions are given on the drug label and no take-back program is available in your area, throw the drugs in the household trash, but first take them out of their original containers and mix them with an undesirable substance, such as used coffee grounds or kitty litter. . . . Put them in a sealable bag, empty can, or other container to prevent the medication from leaking or breaking out of a garbage bag.

FDA's Deputy Director of the Office of Compliance Ilisa Bernstein, Pharm.D., J.D., offers some additional tips:

- Before throwing out a medicine container, scratch out all identifying information on the prescription label to make it unreadable. . . .

- Do not give medications to friends. Doctors prescribe drugs based on a person's specific symptoms and medical history. . . .

- When in doubt about proper disposal, talk to your pharmacist.

"How to Dispose of Unused Medicines," Consumer Updates,
US Department of Health and Human Services,
July 17, 2012. www.fda.gov.

Assessing Takebacks: Little Is Known

Despite their proliferation, little data is available on the impact and effectiveness of takeback programs. In fact, no research has been conducted to investigate takebacks' effect on prescription drug abuse. Though takebacks necessarily reduce the available supply of prescription drugs, voluntary programs are unlikely to draw participation from individuals inclined towards diversion or nonmedical use. While 66 percent of nonmedical users report that friends/relatives were willing participants in diversion, only 4.8 percent obtained drugs from friends/relatives without their permission. Consequently, takebacks may reduce supply without measurably affecting abuse. In addition, . . . most individuals diverting unused drugs originally obtain those drugs from a single doctor, highlighting doctors as the ultimate source of the drug surplus rather than the family medicine cabinet. These data suggest that policy makers may have more success focusing on overprescribing behavior within the medical community rather than on surplus drugs already in individuals' homes. In fact, a study by Simeone Associates Inc. found that states with prescription drug monitoring programs (PDMPs) that proactively monitor prescribing behavior have a lower likelihood of opioid abuse.

Carnevale Associates' analysis found that only 11 percent of the domestic takeback programs surveyed collected data on both costs and medications received. In addition, because of their structure, many programs do not collect controlled substances at all. With few exceptions, those programs that do collect controlled drugs make no effort to determine what percentage of their collections are controlled. To determine takebacks' effectiveness as substance abuse prevention programs, policy makers must know both how much controlled medication they receive and how much the collections cost. Though some programs (notably, Maine's Safe [Medicine] Disposal for ME mailback program) do collect these data, they are not representative of other takebacks and therefore cannot inform a national assessment.

Limited data from our analysis suggest that takebacks' efficiency varies by program characteristics. Our data show that mailback programs cost $62 per pound of collected medication, event-based programs cost $42 per lb., and ongoing bin-based collections cost $7 per lb. Though not statistically significant because of paucity of data, these findings provide a guiding point for future research and real-time policy decisions, indicating that some takeback structures may be considerably more cost-efficient than others.

Recommendations: Further Research

To address these data gaps and help policy makers target limited prevention resources, Carnevale Associates recommends:

- Conducting takeback pilots to determine which medications are collected, assess takebacks' true costs, and link elements of programmatic structure with costs and collections

- Researching the relationship between prescription drug abuse and takeback programs

- Updating the research on PDMPs' contribution to reducing prescription drug abuse and comparing PDMPs to takeback programs

- Focusing takeback resources on the most cost-efficient takebacks until additional data are available

While epidemics often require swift action in advance of research, without these data, takeback programs will remain untested policy. Though potentially useful, such programs may also draw limited prevention resources away from more effective programs, policies, and practices. Similarly, research may link takebacks' effectiveness to certain programmatic features, which may help conserve limited prevention dollars.

Finding a Solution

The prescription drug epidemic is the new frontier of substance abuse policy. Safe and secure disposal of unused medication must be an important component of substance abuse prevention. However, given the dearth of information on takeback programs, more research is needed before heavily investing in takebacks as a key component of substance abuse prevention strategy. Until research can properly assess the effectiveness and cost-effectiveness of takebacks, scarce prevention resources should fund proven policies, programs, and practices, including PDMPs and programs to modify providers' prescribing behavior. Policy makers must seek new solutions to emerging drug problems; however, in these austere times, they must also be careful to allocate scarce prevention dollars to prevention programs that will do the most good.

> *"It's an American catastrophe that has been dubbed pharmageddon, though it rarely pierces the public consciousness. Occasionally a celebrity overdose will attract attention . . . but they are specks in a growing mountain of human mortality."*

An Electronic Prescription Drug Monitoring System Will Guard Against Abuse

Ed Pilkington

Ed Pilkington is the New York correspondent for the Guardian. *In the following viewpoint, he examines the oxycodone problem in Florida, which is considered to be the epicenter of the prescription painkiller problem in the United States. Pilkington reports that the majority of the nation's pill mills, which is the term for pain clinics with little regulation on the prescribing of addictive painkillers, are located in Florida. The epidemic has affected people of all ages and has spurred crime all over the state, according to Pilkington. He finds that activists are battling to introduce an electronic prescription drug monitoring system, which would identify and shut down pill mills and track pa-*

tients who are illegally getting multiple prescriptions for popular painkillers. So far, however, such efforts have been blocked out of concerns over the cost of such a system, Pilkington concludes.

As you read, consider the following questions:

1. According to Pilkington, how many people in Florida died from prescription drug overdoses in 2009?

2. What percentage of the doctors in the United States who handle oxycodone are located in Florida, according to the author?

3. How many health care professionals does the author say were arrested in Palm Beach, Florida, for running pill mills in 2011?

The Kentucky number plate on Chad's pickup truck, parked round the back of a doctor's clinic in Palm Beach, Florida, reveals that he has just driven a thousand miles, 16 hours overnight, to be here—and he's not come for the surfing.

"It's my back," he says, rubbing his lower vertebrae. "I'm a builder. I fell off the roof and hurt my back."

That's odd, as we have just watched him run out of the clinic and over to his truck without so much as a limp. He's clutching a prescription for 180 30 mg [milligram] doses of the painkiller oxycodone.

Pill Mills

Chad is one of thousands of "pillbillies" who descend on Florida every year from across the south and east coasts of America. Some come in trucks bearing telltale number plates from Kentucky, Georgia, Tennessee, even far-away Ohio. Others come by the busload on the apocryphally named Oxycodone Express.

It's a lucrative trade. Chad tells us he has just paid $275 (£168) to the doctor inside the clinic, or pill mill, as it is pejoratively called. The doctor, who can see up to 100 people in a sitting, can make more than $25,000 in a day, cash in hand.

For Chad the profits are handsome too. He will spend $720 at a pharmacy on his 180 pills, giving him a total outlay of about $1,000. Back in Kentucky he can sell each pill for $30, giving them a street value of $5,400 and Chad a clear profit of more than $4,000. If he goes to 10 pill mills in Palm Beach on this one trip he could multiply that windfall tenfold. But then there's the other cost of the oxycodone trade, a cost that is less often talked about, certainly not by Chad or his accommodating doctor.

The Consequences of Prescription Drug Abuse

Every day in Florida seven people die having overdosed on prescription drugs—2,531 died in 2009 alone. That statistic is replicated across the US, where almost 30,000 people died last year [2010] from abusing pharmaceutical pills.

It's an American catastrophe that has been dubbed pharmageddon, though it rarely pierces the public consciousness. Occasionally a celebrity overdose will attract attention—Anna Nicole Smith, Heath Ledger, Michael Jackson—but they are specks in a growing mountain of human mortality.

The White House last month [May 2011] said the abuse of prescription drugs had become the US's fastest-growing drug problem.

Declaring the trend an "alarming public health crisis", it pointed out that people were dying unintentionally from painkiller overdoses at rates that exceeded the crack cocaine epidemic of the 1980s and the black tar heroin epidemic of the 1970s combined.

At the heart of the disaster is the powerfully addictive painkiller oxycodone, which comes in various brands— OxyContin, Roxicodone and Percocet. It is a legitimate therapy

What Is a Prescription Drug Monitoring Program (PDMP)?

A PDMP [prescription drug monitoring program] is a tool that can be used to address prescription drug diversion and abuse. PDMPs serve multiple functions, including: patient care tool; drug epidemic early warning system; and drug diversion and insurance fraud investigative tool. They help prescribers avoid drug interactions and identify drug-seeking behaviors or "doctor shopping." PDMPs can also be used by professional licensing boards to identify clinicians with patterns of inappropriate prescribing and dispensing, and to assist law enforcement in cases of controlled substance diversion.

At the same time, protecting patient privacy is of the utmost importance. PDMPs ensure protection of patient information just as well as, if not better than, any other medical record. Law enforcement may not access patient-specific PDMP data unless they have an active investigation, and health care providers can access only the PDMP data relevant to their patients.

"Prescription Drug Monitoring Programs,"
Office of National Drug Control Policy, April 2011.
www.ncjrs.gov.

for those in great pain but has spawned a generation of addicts and, in turn, attracted crooked doctors who massively expanded the prescription of the drugs in up to 200 pill mills, most in southern Florida.

Victims of the Trend

The epidemic has affected people of all ages but is becoming more prominent among teenagers and young adults.

Ric Bradshaw, the sheriff in Palm Beach, said: "There's a culture that's taking hold among teenagers that because a doctor prescribes these pills they can't be bad. Kids don't have the fear of pharmaceuticals that they do of illegal drugs."

Eleanor Hernandez was introduced to "oxies" when she was 14. "I had no idea it was dangerous at all. Other people were taking it for pain, so why would I worry about it?"

Her mother had just died and Hernandez found that she felt carefree when she took a pill. "It took the pain away, of my mother's death, and physically too. It numbed you, made you feel like you were in a bubble."

By 15 Hernandez was selling oxycodone from the park across the street, making money to pay for her own habit. It was a downward spiral. She was in and out of rehabilitation clinics, in and out of custody. Then she overdosed twice and was resuscitated both times in hospital.

But Hernandez was one of the lucky ones. Now 20, she works in a treatment centre helping 14- to 17-year-olds beat addiction. "To this day I thank God that I found help because if I hadn't I probably wouldn't be here."

A Tragic End

Rich Perry did not find help. He died aged 21 from a cocktail of oxycodone and other prescription and illegal drugs. He began taking prescription pills three years previously, in his last year at high school. He confided in his mother, Karen, that he had a drug problem and went into rehab.

He was clean for a year, but then, without his parents realising, he relapsed, obtaining oxycodone from three separate doctors. He overdosed once but carried on using the drug. The first Karen knew that her son had gone back to the pills was when two officers knocked at her door at 2 A.M. to tell her he was dead.

Electronic Prescription Drug Database

Now, like Hernandez, Perry seeks solace by helping others to avoid her son's fate. She runs the Florida group Narcotics Overdose Prevention and Education—Nope. Together with the American Society of Interventional Pain Physicians it is battling to persuade the state to introduce a monitoring database that would allow police and medical authorities to identify where the oxycodone is coming from, and in turn identify and shut down the pill mills. Though Florida is the epicentre of the oxycodone epidemic, with 98% of all the nation's doctors who handle the drug located here, astonishingly the state has no comprehensive database recording prescription histories.

Even more astonishingly its recently elected governor, the Tea Party favourite Rick Scott, has blocked the introduction of a database on grounds of cost.

That makes Perry see red. "Cost! For heaven's sake! What is the cost of a human life?"

The police are even more baffled. They point out that Florida's lack of regulation has allowed the pill mills to flourish.

The True Cost

Eric Coleman, a narcotics detective in Palm Beach, said the true cost of Florida's oxycodone disaster would surpass that of the database many times over if all costs related to the crisis—state subsidies for prescriptions, policing and incarceration of addicts, hospital visits for those who overdose, autopsies and paupers' burials for the dead—were added up.

The Palm Beach police force has many of the pill mills under surveillance and is steadily shutting them down. Over the past year 33 health care professionals have been arrested in Palm Beach alone and several have had their medical licences revoked.

Yet the police know that until a proper monitoring system is in place, the clampdown they are carrying out will only displace the problem. Pill mills are popping up in other parts of Florida, around Tampa and Orlando, as pill mill doctors move to new pastures.

"This crisis is going to get worse before it gets better," Coleman says. "It's heartbreaking to watch all the families ripped apart, the young lives ended, the damage these doctors—that honourable, esteemed profession that we trust to look after us—are leaving behind."

Periodical and Internet Sources Bibliography

The following articles have been selected to supplement the diverse views presented in this chapter.

Steve Beshear	"Prescription Drug Abuse—No State Is an Island," *Roll Call*, February 26, 2012.
Art Caplan	"It's Time to Hold Doctors Accountable for Painkiller Abuse," NBCNews.com, April 10, 2012.
Jonathan Caulkins	"Parallels with Gun Control," *New York Times*, February 16, 2012.
Damien Cave and Michael S. Schmidt	"Rise in Pill Abuse Forces New Look at U.S. Drug Fight," *New York Times*, July 16, 2012.
Scott Gottlieb	"The DEA's War on Pharmacies—and Pain Patients," *Wall Street Journal*, March 23, 2012.
David Kloth	"America's Fatal Addiction to Prescription Drugs," *Guardian*, June 10, 2011.
Donna Leinwand	"States Target Prescriptions by 'Pill Mills,'" *USA Today*, October 25, 2011.
Greg Risling	"Prescription Pads Play Key Role in Drug Abuse," *San Francisco Chronicle*, May 27, 2012.
Samuel K. Roberts	"Drug Wars Abroad, Prescription Pain Killers at Home," *Huffington Post*, July 12, 2012.
Linda Simoni-Wastila	"A National Monitoring Program," *New York Times*, February 16, 2012.
Telegraph (Hudson, NH)	"Prescription Drug Abuse Gets Congress' Attention," July 22, 2012.
Washington Post	"Maryland Makes the Right Move to Curb Prescription Abuse," April 27, 2011.

CHAPTER 4

What Can Be Done to Help Prevent Prescription Drug Abuse?

Chapter Preface

For years, countries all over the world have struggled to effectively regulate the activities of online pharmacies, also known as Internet pharmacies or mail-order pharmacies. Online pharmacies sell prescription and over-the-counter drugs via the Internet, providing a much-needed convenience for individuals with disabilities or conditions that make it difficult for them to get to a traditional brick-and-mortar pharmacy. Today many insurers and well-known retail pharmacies offer mail-order services for this very reason. In many cases, these online pharmacies may also offer lower prices and other values that appeal to cost-conscious consumers.

However, the ubiquity of rogue online pharmacies has generated much controversy. Critics charge that many of these online pharmacies are scams, sending counterfeit or outdated medications to consumers. Some of these businesses include fraudulent information on their websites and are set up in countries with little or no regulation, allowing them to evade accepted safety protocols. There may not be a pharmacist checking medical histories or for dangerous drug combinations. Many do not require a doctor's prescription to purchase prescription drugs. Minors have been able to purchase illegal prescription drugs—highly addictive and dangerous ones—via the Internet with no safeguards. There is no real confidentiality with these rogue Internet pharmacies, and a consumer's medical records and/or financial information may be compromised and used in criminal acts. Medications have been known to arrive without proper packaging, or shipped without taking care to keep medications at a safe temperature.

In response to growing concerns over online pharmacies and increasing rates of prescription drug abuse, the National Association of Boards of Pharmacy (NABP) developed the Verified Internet Pharmacy Practice Sites (VIPPS) program in

1999. As explicated by NABP, "To be VIPPS accredited, a pharmacy must comply with the licensing and inspection requirements of their state and each state to which they dispense pharmaceuticals. In addition, pharmacies displaying the VIPPS seal have demonstrated to NABP compliance with VIPPS criteria including patient rights to privacy, authentication and security of prescription orders, adherence to a recognized quality assurance policy, and provision of meaningful consultation between patients and pharmacists."

A VIPPS seal displayed on a pharmacy's website ensures that it is not a rogue business and has met all NABP standards. However, some rogue online pharmacies have faked the distinctive VIPPS seal. To counteract this scam, NABP lists all VIPPS-accredited online pharmacies on its website.

It is also important that an online pharmacy be licensed by a legitimate source and located in a country with strong regulations of pharmacies and online businesses. In the United States, online pharmacies are licensed by state boards. Valid online pharmacies will also have an accessible help line, on which consumers can call to speak to a trained health professional. Also, a doctor's prescription should be required to buy prescription-only drugs from an online pharmacy.

The controversy over the best way to regulate online pharmacies to protect consumer safety and curb the problem of prescription drug abuse is one of the issues covered in the following chapter, which examines various measures that can prevent prescription drug abuse. Other viewpoints in the chapter scrutinize patient screening and monitoring practices, the role of parents and doctors in addressing prescription drug abuse, and new technological advances that have impacted the epidemic of prescription painkiller addiction.

> "We find that a step-by-step approach is best for handling patients with complicated pain and potential addiction. It is well described by an airplane analogy: 'We must decide how to land the plane before we take off.'"

Doctors Must Improve Patient Screening and Monitoring to Prevent Prescription Drug Abuse

Murtuza Ghadiali and David Pating

Murtuza Ghadiali and David Pating are supervising addiction medicine physicians at Kaiser Permanente's Chemical Dependency Recovery Program in San Francisco. In the following viewpoint, they express their support for effective pain management strategies but also endorse the "prudent assessment and management of addiction." To that end, Ghadiali and Pating recommend a rigorous screening for substance abuse to see if a patient may be at risk for abuse. They also find it valuable for physicians to document their reasons for prescribing prescription painkillers and monitor compliance, treatment efficacy, and the patient's progress.

Murtuza Ghadiali and David Pating, "The High-Flying Dilemma," *San Francisco Medicine*, April 2012, pp.22–23. Copyright © 2012 by San Francisco Medical Society. All rights reserved. Reproduced by permission.

As you read, consider the following questions:

1. According to the authors, how many overdose deaths from opiates were there in 2011?

2. What state do the authors identify as the leading supplier of OxyContin to the rest of the country?

3. How do the authors describe the function of a SOAPP-5?

For the past two decades, the clinically indicated use of opiates has been framed by two competing mandates: the need to effectively treat pain and the ever-increasing need to prevent addiction and overdose. Beginning in 1995, the newly formed American Pain Society set out guidelines to improve the management of pain, stating, ". . . if pain were assessed with the same zeal as other vital signs are, it would have a much better chance of being treated." In 1999, the Veterans Administration mandated the self-assessment of pain as "the fifth vital sign" in an attempt to improve quality throughout its 1,200 nationwide facilities. Since then, many governmental bodies, including the Medical Board of California (2007), have not only mandated training for the management of pain but have also encouraged physicians to actively treat pain with opiates.

The Growing Demand for Prescription Painkillers

Yet, as the recognition and treatment of acute and chronic pain grows, so too has the demand for prescription opiates. Riding the coattails of this national love affair with pain medication, pharmaceutical companies have obliged the public's demand for opiates by providing a liberal supply of stronger and longer preparations, including the highly abusable opiate OxyContin. OxyContin is now the second-leading drug of abuse in the U.S. Taken together, misuse and abuse of opiates is an unprecedented epidemic, resulting in more than 40,000 overdose deaths in 2011, exceeding the number of annual deaths from auto accidents.

As addiction experts, we see this proliferation of opiates as a major public health problem. This problem has multiple underpinnings. First, the unbridled, consumer-driven demand for opiates has not been balanced by adequate evidence-based pain management strategies. In addressing the "vital sign" of pain, even pain experts do not agree whether opiates are indicated for such conditions such as chronic headaches, fibromyalgia, menstrual cramps, and even nonrheumatoid arthritis, particularly if the real goal of treatment is functional improvement, not just relief from pain. Second, on the supply side, pharmaceuticals have enormous incentive to recoup their deferred drug development investment. When large manufacturers, such as Purdue Pharma [L.P.], makers of OxyContin, hit upon a cash cow, they are amply rewarded with the opportunity to make billions. This, combined with unregulated pharmaceutical sales over the Internet that allow the purchase of non-prescribed opiates with the click of a mouse, has created the current environment: a drug addict's paradise. Florida is now the leading U.S. supplier of OxyContin to the rest of the country, most of it used for nonmedical "recreational" purposes.

The Challenge to Physicians

As addiction physicians charged with helping patients in trouble with the dual issues of pain and addiction, we see a complicated entanglement of different interests in which doctors are caught in the middle. A patient came to us after "being cut off of meds by her doctor." She came with MRI in hand, talking about her need for half a gram of OxyContin a day "just to hug her small child at night." She didn't understand why her family was concerned (although after drinking wine every night with her dinner she was completely

What Can Health Care Practitioners Do?

Most patients take prescription medications responsibly, as directed by their prescribers. However, practitioners must also be aware of the increasing problem with prescription drug abuse. Practitioners prescribing controlled substances can counsel patients to the danger posed by taking these medications in a way not directed for treatment or by combining them with other medications or alcohol. Practitioners can also counsel parents to secure their prescriptions, so that children are not tempted to experiment. And if prescription drugs are left over from a previous condition, patients should properly dispose of them afterward as soon as possible.

"Attention Practitioners! Prescription Drug Abuse Alert: Non-Medical Use of Rx Drugs a Growing Health Crisis," New York State Department of Health, 2006.

incoherent) and why they wanted her to "get help." Our first visit was a long and difficult consult, but it ended in her deciding to come for outpatient addiction treatment and get a chronic pain consult. After consulting with the chronic pain physician, we decided to start buprenorphine for pain, which ended up working well for the patient. The therapists found her very resistant at first but have seen a change in her line of thinking over the course of six weeks. She eventually stabilized on a moderate dose of buprenorphine and feels that her life and pain are more manageable than before.

This case turned out well. Not all do. It's important to remember that opiates are only one modality to treat pain, as is noted in the medical board guidelines for prescribing controlled substances for pain (http://mbc.ca.gov/pain_guide lines.html).

A Step-by-Step Approach

Many times we are asked to consult on cases when either the patient or doctor has become dissatisfied. We find that a step-by-step approach is best for handling patients with complicated pain and potential addiction. It is well described by an airplane analogy: "We must decide how to land the plane before we take off." This translates to our encouraging all physicians to consider, prior to prescribing opiates, 1) whether there is a legitimate condition that warrants use of opiates (a defined destination), 2) whether there are reasonable risks and benefits to prescribing of opiates (takeoff), and 3) whether there are clear requirements for their successful discontinuation (landing).

For patients suspected of or at risk for abuse, prior history or family history of substance abuse is the best clinical predictor of risk at takeoff. When flying high with opiates for acute pain, it is prudent to use the smallest and shortest effective course of opiates. For most acute conditions, two to three weeks is a more than adequate duration of flight. If patients require opiates for two to three months or more, it is prudent to screen for risks of addiction.

At this point, to avoid being labeled zealots, we must remind our colleagues that most patients who are prescribed opiates do not abuse them—most patients will safely discontinue their opiates (auto-land) in reasonable course. Contrariwise, studies do suggest that up to 10 percent of patients *do* misuse their medications. Indications of misuse may include increasing dosage or early refills, reports of lost or stolen medications or frank drug seeking. While some aberrant drug-seeking behavior may result from the undertreatment of pain (aka pseudo-addiction), in our experience the reasons for drug seeking are often unclear and may even include patients who take additional opiates not for pain but for the "stress or coping" with pain.

Again, our motto is: Do not fly a plane that you cannot land.

SOAPP-5

For patients who need opiates for more than two to three months or if you are in the transitional no-man's-land between acute and chronic pain, a SOAPP-5 (Screener and Opiate Assessment for People with Pain) is a good compass to fly by. SOAPP-5 is a five-item questionnaire that helps assess, on a scale of 0 to 4, the potential for opiate misuse. Patients with SOAPP-5 $\geq$ 4 have high potential for abuse and should be given a shorter leash or monitored more frequently.

If a patient manifests aberrant behaviors, we recommend an early consultation with a chronic pain physician. It's important to be descriptive of the behavior without making a stigmatizing diagnosis unless one is certain (e.g., diagnosing addiction for an early refill or lost prescription or taking more than prescribed). Pain contracts using the universal precautions for pain management (e.g., regular screening for addiction and good documentation) are also helpful. If you suspect an addiction, a referral to an addiction medicine specialist is essential to determine who might safely stay on opiates as long as they capably treat and manage their addiction. Addiction is characterized by the loss of control and compulsion to use the drug and not simply withdrawal and tolerance. Lastly, urine toxicology adds little to the picture, except when you need to prove the patient is taking opiate medications as prescribed (and not selling or giving them away), or to make sure they are not abusing other recreational drugs.

In summary, we support the effective management of pain, but we also endorse the prudent assessment and management of the risk of addiction. For the one in ten individuals who may misuse or abuse their opiates, we recommend screening for substance abuse or family history of abuse, or more formally using the SOAPP-5 tool. Most importantly, we encourage our colleagues who treat acute and chronic pain to document their reasoning for initiating opiates and to continually demonstrate their prudence by monitoring compliance, treatment efficacy, and the achievement of functional improvement.

| "*Measures are necessary to address the availability of these drugs on the Internet and increase physician awareness of the dangers posed by Internet pharmacies.*"

Physicians Must Warn Patients About the Dangers of Online Pharmacies

Rick Nauert

Rick Nauert is the senior news editor of PsychCentral. In the following viewpoint, he finds that many US physicians are unaware of the availability of controlled substances over the Internet. With the abuse of prescription drugs a growing and persistent issue, Nauert explains, physicians need to play a central role in addressing the challenges posed by Internet pharmacies. Nauert argues that physicians should be incorporating questioning about Internet-based medication use with their patients and must educate them about the risks of purchasing drugs online.

Rick Nauert, "Prescription Drug Abuse Aided by Internet Pharmacies, MD Ignorance," PsychCentral, December 20, 2011. Copyright © 2011 by Psych Central. All rights reserved. Reproduced by permission.

As you read, consider the following questions:

1. What percentage of websites offering controlled prescription drugs do not require a prescription, according to recent studies cited in the viewpoint?

2. What percentage of prescription drug abusers do studies suggest purchase their drugs online, according to Nauert?

3. According to a study cited by Nauert, what happened with every 10 percent increase in high-speed Internet use from 2000 to 2007?

A buse of prescription drugs has reached epidemic levels, yet many physicians are often unaware of the availability of controlled substances over the Internet.

In a commentary in the journal *Annals of Internal Medicine*, investigators describe the probable contribution of Internet pharmacies to the problem and outline potential strategies for addressing it.

The Role of the Internet

Experts say awareness and new policies to combat the trade are critical to halt the growing abuse of prescription drugs. Measures are necessary to address the availability of these drugs on the Internet and increase physician awareness of the dangers posed by Internet pharmacies.

"Controlled prescription drugs like OxyContin, Xanax, and Ritalin are easily purchased over the Internet without a prescription, yet physician awareness of this problem is low," says Anupam B. Jena, M.D., Ph.D., lead author of the article.

"Abuse of medications purchased from websites can pose unique challenges to physicians because patients who abuse these medications may not fit clinical stereotypes of drug abusers."

The Prescription Drug Abuse Epidemic

The authors note that abuse of controlled prescription drugs now exceeds abuse of all illegal drugs combined, except marijuana. In November [2011], the U.S. Centers for Disease Control and Prevention reported that the death toll from overdoses of prescription painkillers such as OxyContin has more than tripled in the past decade.

Some illegitimate online pharmacies sell drugs with no prescription or medical information at all while others ask for completion of a questionnaire before a prescription is issued by a physician who has never seen the patient.

Studies have found that 85 percent of websites offering controlled prescription drugs do not require a prescription, and many that do allow the prescription to be faxed, increasing the risk of forgery or fraud.

"The Internet serves as an open channel for distribution of controlled prescription drugs with no mechanisms to even block sales to children. This is particularly dangerous given that addiction is a disease that, in most cases, originates with substance use in adolescence," said Susan Foster, M.S.W., of the National Center on Addiction and Substance Abuse at Columbia University, which contributed to the commentary.

An Incomplete Picture

Additional investigations by U.S. agencies have verified the ease with which controlled drugs can be purchased online, but little information is available on how drugs acquired that way are used.

While some surveys suggest that as many as 10 percent of prescription drug abusers obtain their drugs online, the authors stress that such surveys probably underestimate the situation and would not reach individuals most likely to abuse prescription drugs purchased over the Internet.

"Be the first of your friends to like this." Cartoon by Kjell Maki. www.CartoonStock .com.

They also note that surveys in drug treatment centers would totally miss local drug dealers, who are increasingly likely to access their supplies online.

Earlier this year Jena and Dana Goldman, Ph.D., director of the [Leonard D.] Schaeffer Center [for Health Policy and

Economics] at USC [the University of Southern California] and a co-author of the commentary, published a study finding that states with the greatest expansion in high-speed Internet access from 2000 to 2007 also had the largest increase in admissions for treatment of prescription drug abuse.

They estimated that for every 10 percent increase in high-speed Internet use during those years, admissions for prescription drug abuse increased 1 percent.

The Role of Physicians

"Prescription use starts with the physician," said Goldman, "and we need to more actively engage them to control illicit use. Access to universal, electronic prescription records would be of great assistance in this regard."

Both federal and private agencies have taken measures to reduce the impact of illicit Internet pharmacies, including the 2008 passage of the Ryan Haight Online Pharmacy Consumer Protection Act, which specifically prohibits delivery of controlled substances prescribed by a physician who had never examined the patient.

But it is not known whether that law and related efforts, such as FDA [Food and Drug Administration] warning letters to Internet pharmacies and their service providers, are at all successful. The authors note that regulatory efforts also are "stymied by these pharmacies' ability to appear, disappear, and reappear constantly," and the reluctance of search engines to stop running ads for rogue online pharmacies.

The increasing online availability of prescription drugs may entice individuals believed to be at low risk for drug abuse to overuse controlled medications.

The authors note that, while physicians and other health care providers should play a major part in addressing the challenges posed by Internet pharmacies, their awareness of the problem and ability to recognize and treat substance abuse of any kind is usually limited.

"Physicians need to educate patients about the risks of purchasing any medications over the Internet and should consider brief but routine questioning about Internet-based medication use," said Jena [Goldman]. "Given the ability of illegal online pharmacies to evade law enforcement efforts, physician awareness and involvement will be crucial to reducing this problem."

> *"Although most medical negligence cases are handled in civil court, the recent conviction of Michael Jackson's doctor for involuntary manslaughter reflects the growing belief that a stronger deterrent is needed, and in some cases, doctors should be held criminally liable when their patients abuse and overdose on prescription drugs."*

Doctors Who Enable or Facilitate Prescription Drug Overdose Should Be Criminally Prosecuted

Erica Trachtman

Erica Trachtman is a law student. In the following viewpoint, she examines the controversy surrounding physicians charged in criminal courts for patients' prescription overdoses. As an example, she turns to the 2011 case of Dr. Conrad Murray, who was convicted of involuntary manslaughter in the death of superstar Michael Jackson. Trachtman concedes that such prosecutions may have a chilling effect on the treatment of chronic pain,

Erica Trachtman, "Prescription Drug Abuse Aided by Internet Pharmacies, MD Ignorance," *American Criminal Law Review*, December 20, 2011. Copyright © 2011 by Georgetown Law. All rights reserved. Reproduced by permission.

but she argues that pursuing criminal liability against negligent, greedy, or incompetent physicians may be the best deterrent to physicians abandoning their ethical responsibilities.

As you read, consider the following questions:

1. According to the Drug Enforcement Administration (DEA), how many successful criminal prosecutions of physicians were there for negligently prescribing medication in 2008?

2. How many years does Trachtman report that Dr. Conrad Murray received for his conviction for involuntary manslaughter in the death of Michael Jackson?

3. In what year did more people die from narcotic drugs than in car crashes for the first time in US history, according to the author?

On Saturday, February 18, 2012, a crowd gathered at the New Hope Baptist Church in Newark, New Jersey, to mourn the untimely loss of music legend Whitney Houston. Although the results of a toxicology test are still weeks away, preliminary reports cite a deadly mixture of alcohol and prescription drugs as the cause of Houston's death. Multiple prescription drugs were found in the Beverly Hills hotel room where Houston died, including Xanax. It is no secret that the singer had struggled with substance abuse problems for years, but to what extent should her doctor be held accountable for her death? The physicians of the rich and famous regularly face the temptation to ignore ethical obligations and acquiesce to the unreasonable demands of their patients. Although most medical negligence cases are handled in civil court, the recent conviction of Michael Jackson's doctor for involuntary manslaughter reflects the growing belief that a stronger deterrent is needed, and in some cases, doctors should be held criminally liable when their patients abuse and overdose on prescription drugs.

According to the Centers for Disease Control and Prevention, fatal overdoses from prescription drugs more than tripled to 13,800 in the United States in 1999 through 2006. Physicians typically face civil liability for the death of a patient, with the victim's family suing for monetary damages. Physicians, however, can also be convicted for the death of a patient by prescription drug overdose under the Controlled Substances Act, a parallel state version of the act, or a state homicide statute. Despite opposition from the American Medical Association that the tort system is sufficient for holding doctors accountable for negligently prescribing medication, the Drug Enforcement Administration reports a steady rise in successful criminal prosecutions of physicians, from just 15 convictions in 2003 to 43 in 2008. Perhaps the most infamous prosecution of a physician occurred just last year [in 2011].

The Michael Jackson Tragedy

Back in June 2009, the world was stunned and devastated by the sudden death of Michael Jackson. As the investigation surrounding his death unfolded, millions of the King of Pop's fans quickly learned a name they would not soon forget: Dr. Conrad Murray. Dr. Murray was a cardiologist who became Jackson's personal physician in early 2009, a position that earned him a cushy six-figure monthly salary. Dr. Murray left his medical practice in Las Vegas and was planning to accompany Jackson on his international tour later that summer. Jackson reportedly struggled with chronic insomnia, and Dr. Murray was willing to provide the cure: propofol, an intravenous anesthesia used during surgical procedures. Just a few hours before his death, Dr. Murray gave Jackson a 25 mg [milligram] injection of propofol (in addition to several other previously administered drugs); Jackson allegedly had pleaded for the drug incessantly for several hours. When Dr. Murray later discovered that Jackson was not breathing, he attempted

CPR and administered another drug which can serve as an antidote for certain overdoses. But just two hours later, Jackson was pronounced dead.

The Los Angeles County coroner eventually classified Jackson's death as a homicide. Specifically, the coroner concluded that Jackson's death was caused by "acute propofol intoxication." Jackson allegedly had sought propofol from three other medical professionals; however, all had refused because the drug is intended for sedation during surgical procedures and is not approved for at-home insomnia treatment. The Food and Drug Administration requires that propofol be administered only by physicians trained in general anesthesia.

Dr. Murray was convicted in the Los Angeles County Superior Court of involuntary manslaughter for what the presiding judge described as a "horrific violation of trust." He is sentenced to four years' imprisonment, the maximum sentence allowed under the law. Central to the government's case was Murray's willingness to administer the anesthesia in an unmonitored setting, his failure to resuscitate Jackson properly, and the lack of records he kept for Jackson's treatment. The Jackson family issued a statement, which was read to the court during sentencing proceedings; they requested a sentence that "reminds physicians that they cannot sell their services to the highest bidder and cast aside their Hippocratic oath to do no harm."

Although Dr. Murray probably will never practice medicine again and will have to endure the stigma of the conviction for the rest of his life, he may yet profit from this troubling chapter of his life. The Jackson family instructed prosecutors to withdraw a request for Murray to pay over $100 million in restitution. Wrongful death suits also are pending against AEC Live, the company that promoted Jackson's planned concerts, not Dr. Murray. As a result, he probably will keep any money he earns from movie or book deals, notwithstanding the fact that he chose money over his moral obligations as a doctor. So, is criminal prosecution really the answer?

The Controlled Substances Act (CSA)

Enacted in 1970, the Controlled Substances Act (CSA), 28 U.S.C. § 801, regulates the manufacture and distribution of drugs. In order to prescribe controlled substances, physicians must register with the Drug Enforcement Administration. In addition, the CSA requires physicians to adhere to specific prescription guidelines. Prescriptions must be dated and include the name and address of both the patient and the prescribing doctor. To establish guilt, the prosecution must prove that the physician knowingly and intentionally prescribed the medication outside "the usual course of professional practice" or not for a "legitimate medical purpose." Violations of any part of the CSA can result in fines and/or imprisonment.

Anna Nicole Smith's physician, Sandeep Kapoor, was charged, but ultimately acquitted of violating the California controlled substances law. The case came down to whether Kapoor believed in good faith that there was a medical purpose for providing Smith with an array of prescription drugs that led to her overdose and death in 2007. Interestingly, while Kapoor walked away a free man, successful prosecutions were brought against Smith's boyfriend and psychiatrist for using false names on her prescriptions.

Typically, in response to violations of the CSA or an equivalent state statute, state medical boards will temporarily suspend medical licenses or place doctors on probation. If a physician is convicted under a state homicide statute, however, his license is permanently revoked. Thus, in particularly egregious or highly publicized cases, pursuing a homicide charge becomes the more enticing option. Physicians in these cases are usually tried under a charge of involuntary manslaughter, which does not require a showing of malice.

Is Conviction the Right Option?

While there has not been a substantial number of criminal malpractice cases, the American Medical Association worries that the trend has interfered with the practice of medicine. In 1995, the group adopted a resolution opposing the "attempted criminalization of health care decision making especially as represented by the current trend toward the criminalization of malpractice."

Undoubtedly such prosecutions have a chilling effect on the willingness of doctors to prescribe some necessary medication for the legitimate pain of patients. But in 2009, for the first time in U.S. history, more people died from narcotic drugs than in car crashes. Abuse of prescription drugs was largely to blame. The role of the prescribing physician(s) in Whitney Houston's case remains to be seen, but already several doctors' offices and pharmacies have been subpoenaed for their records. As long as there are patients willing to pay, physicians will be tempted to become their personal black market pharmacists. Thus, the imposition of criminal liability on top of civil liability may be the best deterrent to preventing physicians from taking advantage of their role as trusted caregivers and prescribing unnecessary drugs.

"Set clear rules for teens about all drug use, including not sharing medicine and always following the medical provider's advice and dosages."

Parents Can Be Critical in the Prevention of Teen Prescription Drug Abuse

Parents. The Anti-Drug

Parents. The Anti-Drug is the website of the National Youth Anti-Drug Media Campaign, which is run by the Office of National Drug Control Policy (ONDCP). In the following viewpoint, the author underscores the central role parents have in keeping their teenage children drug free. The author lists a number of key actions parents can take, including safeguarding and monitoring all existing drugs at home; setting clear rules with teenagers; being a good role model; and properly concealing and disposing of old medicines in the trash. It is imperative, the author asserts, for parents to warn teens about the dangers of abusing prescription and over-the-counter (OTC) drugs.

As you read, consider the following questions:

1. What specific ways does the author suggest parents monitor all prescription drugs in the home?

"Preventing Rx Drug Abuse," Parents. The Anti-Drug, Whitehouse.gov, January 31, 2008.

2. How does the author recommend that parents set a good example for their kids?

3. What undesirable substances does the author suggest that parents mix prescription drugs with when thrown in the trash?

Think about your home. What prescription and over-the-counter (OTC) drugs do you have? Where are they kept? Would you know if some were missing? The good news is that you can take steps immediately to limit access to these drugs and help keep your teen drug free:

1. *Safeguard all drugs at home. Monitor quantities and control access.* Take note of how many pills are in a bottle or pill packet, and keep track of refills. This goes for your own medication, as well as for your teen and other members of your household. If you find you have to refill medication more often than expected, there could be a real problem—someone may be taking your medication without your knowledge. If your teen has been prescribed a drug, be sure you control the medication, and monitor dosages and refills.

2. *Set clear rules for teens about all drug use, including not sharing medicine and always following the medical provider's advice and dosages.* Make sure your teen uses prescription drugs only as directed by a medical provider and follows instructions for OTC products carefully. This includes taking the proper dosage and not using with other substances without a medical provider's approval. Teens should never take prescription or OTC drugs with street drugs or alcohol. If you have any questions about how to take a drug, call your family physician or pharmacist.

3. *Be a good role model by following these same rules with your own medicines.* Examine your own behavior to ensure you set a good example. If you misuse your prescription drugs, such as share them with your kids, or abuse them, your teen

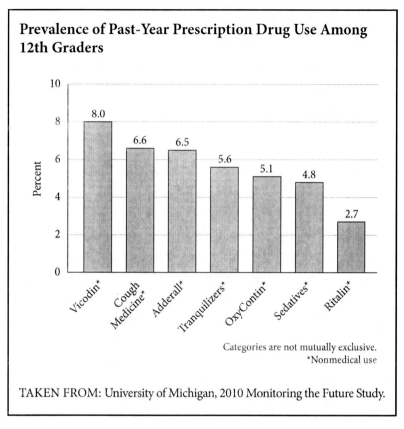

Prevalence of Past-Year Prescription Drug Use Among 12th Graders

Categories are not mutually exclusive.
*Nonmedical use

TAKEN FROM: University of Michigan, 2010 Monitoring the Future Study.

will take notice. Avoid sharing your drugs and always follow your medical provider's instructions.

Proper Disposal Is Key

4. *Properly conceal and dispose of old or unneeded medicines in the trash.* Unneeded prescription drugs should be hidden and thrown away in the trash. So that teens or others don't take them out of the trash, you can mix them with an undesirable substance (like used coffee grounds or kitty litter) and put the mixture in an empty can or bag. Unless the directions say otherwise, do NOT flush medications down the drain or toilet because the chemicals can pollute the water supply. Also, remove any personal, identifiable information from prescription bottles or pill packages before you throw them away.

5. *Ask friends and family to safeguard their prescription drugs as well.* Make sure your friends and relatives, especially grandparents, know about the risks, too, and encourage them to regularly monitor their own medicine cabinets. If there are other households your teen has access to, talk to those families as well about the importance of safeguarding medications. If you don't know the parents of your child's friends, then make an effort to get to know them, and get on the same page about rules and expectations for use of all drugs, including alcohol and illicit drugs. Follow up with your teen's school administration to find out what they are doing to address issues of prescription and over-the-counter drug abuse in schools.

Talk to your teen about the dangers of abusing prescription and over-the-counter drugs. These are powerful drugs that, when abused, can be just as dangerous as street drugs. Tell your teen the risks far outweigh any "benefits."

> "Educating prescribers on substance abuse is critically important, because even brief interventions by primary care providers have proven effective in reducing or eliminating substance abuse in people who abuse drugs but are not yet addicted to them."

Education Is Key in Fighting Prescription Drug Abuse

Office of National Drug Control Policy

The Office of National Drug Control Policy (ONDCP) is a US government agency that advises President Barack Obama on federal drug policy and formulates national drug control strategies. In the following viewpoint, the ONDCP elucidates the central role education plays in tackling the problem of prescription drug abuse, calling it a "crucial first step." The ONDCP maintains that parents and children need to be better educated about the dangers of prescription drug abuse. Health care professionals—including physicians, dentists, pharmacists, and nurses—should be receiving more training on diagnosing and preventing the problem, the ONDCP contends. The ONDCP outlines spe-

"Epidemic: Responding to America's Prescription Drug Abuse Crisis," Office of National Drug Control Policy, Whitehouse.gov, 2011.

cific action items that will be taken at the national level to improve efforts as well as to increase research and development in the area of prescription drug abuse.

As you read, consider the following questions:

1. What did the ONDCP learn about the prevalence of substance use disorder training in medical residency programs in 2008?

2. What role does the ONDCP see the American College of Emergency Physicians playing in educating health care providers about prescription drug abuse?

3. What role does the ONDCP see prescription drug manufacturers playing in parent, youth, and patient education?

A crucial first step in tackling the problem of prescription drug abuse is to raise awareness through the education of parents, youths, patients, and health care providers. Although there have been great strides in raising awareness about the dangers of using illegal drugs, many people are still not aware that the misuse or abuse of prescription drugs can be as dangerous as the use of illegal drugs, leading to addiction and even death.

The Vital Role of Education

Parents and youths in particular need to be better educated about the dangers of the misuse and abuse of prescription drugs. There is a common misperception among many parents and youths that prescription drugs are less dangerous when abused than illegal drugs because they are FDA [Food and Drug Administration]-approved. Many well-meaning parents do not understand the risks associated with giving prescribed medication to a teenager or another family member for whom the medication was not prescribed. Many parents are also not aware that youths are abusing prescription drugs; thus, they frequently leave unused prescription drugs in open medicine cabinets while making sure to lock their liquor cabinets. These misperceptions, coupled with increased direct-to-consumer advertising, which may also contribute to increased demand for medications, makes effective educational programs even more vital to combating prescription drug abuse.

In addition, prescribers and dispensers, including physicians, physicians' assistants, nurse practitioners, pharmacists, nurses, prescribing psychologists, and dentists, all have a role to play in reducing prescription drug misuse and abuse. Most receive little training on the importance of appropriate prescribing and dispensing of opioids to prevent adverse effects, diversion, and addiction. Outside of specialty addiction treatment programs, most health care providers have received minimal training in how to recognize substance abuse in their patients. Most medical, dental, pharmacy, and other health professional schools do not provide in-depth training on substance abuse; often, substance abuse education is limited to classroom or clinical electives. Moreover, students in these schools may only receive limited training on treating pain.

Substance Use Disorder Training

A national survey of medical residency programs in 2000 found that, of the programs studied, only 56 percent required substance use disorder training, and the number of curricular hours in the required programs varied between 3 to 12 hours. A 2008 follow-up survey found that some progress has been made to improve medical school, residency, and post-residency substance abuse education; however, these efforts have not been uniformly applied in all residency programs or medical schools.

Educating prescribers on substance abuse is critically important, because even brief interventions by primary care providers have proven effective in reducing or eliminating sub-

How Should the Public Be Educated?

The most important aspect of the training is for the public. The public must be educated on non-opiate techniques of chronic pain management. In addition, the public should be educated about the overall ineffectiveness of opioid use, prevalence of misuse and adverse effects, even if used properly. Further, public education should include youth and family education, prevention strategies specific for people with access to controlled prescription drugs with media campaigns, community coalitions, . . . prescription drug tracking, prevention and intervention by biometric identification at various levels, students and employees, etc.; screening, brief intervention, referral and treatment.

Laxmaiah Manchikanti, "National Drug Control Policy and Prescription Drug Abuse: Facts and Fallacies," Pain Physician, vol. 10, no. 3, May 2007.

stance abuse in people who abuse drugs but are not yet addicted to them. In addition, educating health care providers about prescription drug abuse will promote awareness of this growing problem among prescribers so they will not overprescribe the medication necessary to treat minor conditions. This, in turn, will reduce the amount of unused medication sitting in medicine cabinets in homes across the country.

The following action items will be taken to improve educational efforts and to increase research and development:

Health Care Provider Education

- Work with Congress to amend federal law to require practitioners (such as physicians, dentists, and others authorized to prescribe) who request DEA [Drug Enforcement Administration] registration to prescribe controlled substances to be trained on responsible opioid prescribing practices as a precondition of registration. This training would include assessing and addressing signs of abuse and/or dependence.

- Require drug manufacturers, through the Opioid Risk Evaluation and Mitigation Strategy (REMS), to develop effective educational materials and initiatives to train practitioners on the appropriate use of opioid pain relievers.

- Federal agencies that support their own health care systems will increase continuing education for their practitioners and other health care providers on proper prescribing and disposal of prescription drugs.

- Work with appropriate medical and health care boards to encourage them to require education curricula in health professional schools (medical, nursing, pharmacy, and dental) and continuing education programs to include instruction on the safe and appropriate use of opioids to treat pain while minimizing the risk of addiction and substance abuse. Additionally, work with relevant medical, nursing, dental, and pharmacy student groups to help disseminate educational materials, and establish student programs that can give community educational presentations on prescription drug abuse and substance abuse.

- In consultation with medical specialty organizations, develop methods of assessing the adequacy and effectiveness of pain treatment in patients and in patient populations, to better inform the appropriate use of opioid pain medications.

- Work with the American College of Emergency Physicians to develop evidence-based clinical guidelines that establish best practices for opioid prescribing in the Emergency Department.

- Work with all stakeholders to develop tools to facilitate appropriate opioid prescribing, including development of patient-provider agreements and guidelines.

Parent, Youth, and Patient Education

- Enlist all stakeholders to support and promote an evidence-based public education campaign on the appropriate use, secure storage, and disposal of prescription drugs, especially controlled substances. Engage local antidrug coalitions, and other organizations (chain pharmacies, community pharmacies, boards of pharmacies, boards of medicine) to promote and disseminate public education materials and to increase awareness of prescription drug misuse and abuse.

- Require manufacturers, through the Opioid Risk Evaluation and Mitigation Strategy (REMS), to develop effective educational materials for patients on the appropriate use and disposal of opioid pain relievers.

- Working with private sector groups, develop an evidence-based media campaign on prescription drug abuse, targeted to parents, in an effort to educate them about the risks associated with prescription drug abuse and the importance of secure storage and proper disposal of prescription drugs (including through public alerts or other approaches to capture the attention of busy parents).

Research and Development

- Expedite research, through grants, partnerships with academic institutions, and priority new drug application review by the FDA, on the development of treatments for pain with no abuse potential as well as on the development of abuse-deterrent formulations (ADF) of opioid medications and other drugs with abuse potential.

• Continue advancing the design and evaluation of epidemiological studies to address changing patterns of abuse.

• Provide guidance to the pharmaceutical industry on the development of abuse-deterrent drug formulations and on post-market assessment of their performance.

> *"Many pharmaceutical companies have made strides in tackling what the U.S. Centers for Disease Control and Prevention calls a national epidemic."*

New Technology Can Make Prescription Drugs More Difficult to Abuse

Marni Jameson

Marni Jameson is a reporter for the Orlando Sentinel. *In the following viewpoint, she reports on recent efforts by pharmaceutical companies to develop new technologies to make prescription drugs difficult to abuse. Jameson describes several of these new technologies, including Aversion, which makes a pill physically irritating to nasal passages when abusers crush and snort it. Another technology, known as Impede, cuts the yield of methamphetamine abusers can extract from nasal decongestants such as Sudafed, she explains. Jameson contends that these emerging technologies are just one part of a broad campaign to fight prescription drug abuse.*

As you read, consider the following questions:

1. What does Jameson cite as the main focus of the National Rx Drug Abuse Summit in Orlando, Florida, in 2012?

2. According to the US Centers for Disease Control and Prevention (CDC), how many Americans die of a drug overdose every nineteen minutes?

3. What product does Jameson say was the first to incorporate Aversion technology?

As the nation's leaders in the war against prescription drug abuse met this week [April 10–12, 2012] in Orlando, scientists in labs across the country continued efforts to make the most abused drugs "unabusable."

Although much of the National Rx Drug Abuse Summit focused on what government agencies, law enforcement officials and medical practitioners can do to curtail abuse, those leading key summit sessions acknowledged that pharmaceutical science may offer the best remedy yet.

Creating a Drug That Can't Be Abused

Reformulating commonly abused drugs in novel ways that reduce abuse needs to be part of the solution, said Nora Volkow, director of the National Institute on Drug Abuse, in a keynote address at the three-day conference, which ended Thursday.

Many pharmaceutical companies have made strides in tackling what the U.S. Centers for Disease Control and Prevention [CDC] calls a national epidemic, say industry experts. One American dies of a drug overdose every 19 minutes, according to the CDC.

Common deterrents for misuse include foiling the ways abusers tamper with pills. Two years ago, Purdue Pharma [L.P.], based in Stamford, Conn., released a new version of the painkiller oxycodone that defies crushing and cutting, common ways drug abusers tamper with the prescription drug to enhance its effect.

"It's still a tablet," said Libby Holman, spokeswoman for the pharmaceutical. "We've just made it harder to misuse and abuse, by making it much more difficult to prepare for snorting or injecting."

More Technologies

Acura Pharmaceuticals has developed two technologies to slow down abusers, said CEO Bob Jones. One is by incorporating a polymer that, when an abuser tries to dissolve the drug to inject, turns the product to gel so it won't go through a needle.

The second way is by formulating the product so that when it's crushed and snorted it creates such intense nasal irritation that "abusers won't want to do it twice," said Jones.

That technology, called Aversion, has debuted in its first FDA [Food and Drug Administration]-approved application in Oxecta, an immediate-release oxycodone product. The company plans to extend the application to other, even more widely prescribed painkillers, such as Percocet and Vicodin, said Jones.

Impede Technology

The company's Impede technology limits how much methamphetamine abusers can extract from pseudoephedrine, a common over-the-counter nasal decongestant sold as Sudafed.

Abusers use the household cold remedy to cook up methamphetamine in makeshift home labs, said Jones. Impede cuts the yield in half, said Jones, for the product that is not yet on the market.

Gummy Bear Drugs

Other unabusable drug methods companies are using include creating pills that are the consistency of gummy bears, so too soft to crush, or that have particles too tiny to crush, said Jones. Other drugs are being reformulated so they won't work unless they come in contact with digestive enzymes in the stomach.

"They must break down in the gut, so they're useless if snorted or injected," he said. Others release an agent when crushed that makes them impotent.

Although many pharmaceutical representatives, including one from Purdue, attended the summit, none presented or exhibited, said Dale Morton, conference spokesman. "We deliberately avoided pharma money because we didn't want there to be any appearance that this meeting was biased in any way. Many consider pharmaceutical companies to be part of the problem."

One Step in a Broad Anti-Abuse Plan

Although those who attended the summit see companies creating new drug formulas as part of the solution, many other parties will also need to take an active role, said Morton. Doctors, the government, pharmacies, distributors, law enforcement, the insurance industry and public health educators all need to get involved.

"We won't change human nature by mixing a few ingredients into our tablets," said Jones, of the pharma labs' collective efforts. "But if we make some headway, we can keep people out of the hospital and out of the morgue.

"This is the right thing to do."

Periodical and Internet Sources Bibliography

The following articles have been selected to supplement the diverse views presented in this chapter.

Carol J. Boyd	"Patients Must Also Be Responsible," *New York Times*, February 16, 2012.
Michael Cook	"Abolish the Prescription Drug System, Says Bioethicist," *BioEdge*, August 1, 2012.
Economist	"Pills and Progress," February 11, 2012.
Calvina Fay	"Public Education Campaigns," *New York Times*, February 16, 2012.
FoxNews.com	"Doctors Call for New U.S. Painkiller Labels to Stop Abuse," July 26, 2012.
Alexander Gaffney	"Sen. Feinstein Introduces Bill to Regulate Online Pharmacies," *Regulatory Focus*, December 28, 2011.
Will James	"Report Faults Doctors," *Wall Street Journal*, May 25, 2012.
Timothy W. Martin	"Group Asks FDA to Provide Clearer Painkiller Guidelines," *Wall Street Journal*, July 25, 2012.
Timothy W. Martin	"Ohio Tries High-Tech Tactics to Fight Painkiller Abuse," *Wall Street Journal*, July 27, 2012.
Sharon Meieran	"Fighting Prescription Drug Abuse, While Treating Pain, Is a Health Care Crisis," *Oregonian*, July 2, 2012.
Katie Moisse	"Abuse-Proof Prescription Painkillers May Spur Heroin Habit," ABCNews.com, July 11, 2012.
Kevin A. Sabet	"How to Treat the Epidemic," *New York Times*, February 15, 2012.

For Further Discussion

Chapter 1

1. In her viewpoint, Monifa Thomas maintains that there is an epidemic of prescription painkiller abuse in the United States. Radley Balko argues that the evidence that there is a prescription painkiller abuse epidemic is inconclusive. Which writer makes the more persuasive argument, and why?

2. Do you believe that driving while under the influence of prescription drugs is a growing problem? Read viewpoints by the National Institute on Drug Abuse and Angel Streeter to inform your answer.

3. "Pharm parties" have been identified as a troubling teen trend. In his viewpoint, Jeff Mosier describes the threat. Jack Shafer, however, debunks the trend as a myth in his viewpoint. Do you think "pharm parties" exist? Identify the argument you think is more effective and explain your reasoning.

Chapter 2

1. What do you think is the connection between chronic pain and prescription painkiller abuse? Read viewpoints written by Liz Szabo and Miranda Hitti to inform your answer.

2. This chapter surveys some of the major causes of prescription drug abuse. Which do think is the most important? Which seems like the most difficult to address? Explain your reasoning.

Chapter 3

1. What should be the role of government in fighting prescription drug abuse? Read the viewpoints in the chapter to inform your answer.

2. The issue of decriminalizing drugs is very controversial. Read viewpoints by David Rosen and William J. Bennett to learn about both sides of the issue. Should prescription drugs be decriminalized? Why or why not? Explain.

3. Ed Pilkington contends that an electronic prescription drug monitoring system would be very effective in tracking drug abusers and doctors who overprescribe medications. What is your opinion on such a system? Do you think such a system would violate patient privacy? If so, how? Which do you think is more important: monitoring patient prescriptions or protecting patient privacy? Explain your reasoning.

Chapter 4

1. The first two viewpoints of this chapter explore the role of doctors in preventing prescription drug abuse. After reading the viewpoints, how do you think physicians can be more effective in preventing prescription drug addiction? Use examples from the text to inform your answer.

2. Erica Trachtman argues that doctors should be prosecuted if they facilitate prescription drug abuse. Do you agree or disagree with her opinion? Explain your answer.

Organizations to Contact

The editors have compiled the following list of organizations concerned with the issues debated in this book. The descriptions are derived from materials provided by the organizations. All have publications or information available for interested readers. The list was compiled on the date of publication of the present volume; the information provided here may change. Be aware that many organizations take several weeks or longer to respond to inquiries, so allow as much time as possible.

Centers for Disease Control and Prevention (CDC)
1600 Clifton Road, Atlanta, GA   30333
(800) 232-4636
e-mail: cdcinfo@cdc.gov
website: www.cdc.gov

The Centers for Disease Control and Prevention (CDC) is the US government agency responsible for monitoring the nation's health and investigating health problems and disease outbreaks. The CDC also works to develop and implement sound health policies, which derive from comprehensive research, surveys, and collaboration with local, regional, and national partners. The CDC promotes healthy behaviors and emphasizes disease prevention. To educate the public on prescription drug abuse, the CDC created a website, Prescription Drug Overdoses: State Laws, that surveys state strategies to regulate prescription drug use and fight abuse. The CDC website features vital information on the agency's work, including podcasts and blogs that cover recent initiatives and activities. It also offers access to a range of publications, including *Emerging Infectious Diseases Journal* and the *Morbidity and Mortality Weekly Report*.

Department of Health and Human Services (HHS)
200 Independence Avenue SW, Washington, DC   20201
(877) 696-6775
website: www.hhs.gov

The Department of Health and Human Services (HHS) is the US government agency in charge of protecting the health of and providing essential health services to all Americans. HHS works closely with state and local governments to develop programs and implement policies. It is the goal of the HHS to have a variety of safe and effective pain relievers for Americans and to provide accurate and up-to-date research on prescription drugs. The HHS website offers a series of fact sheets on different prescription drug options and information on fighting prescription drug abuse.

Drug Enforcement Administration (DEA)
Mailstop: AES, 8701 Morrissette Drive, Springfield, VA 22152
(202) 307-1000
website: www.dea.gov

The Drug Enforcement Administration (DEA) is a division within the US Department of Justice that focuses on enforcing the nation's drug laws and reducing the amount of illegal drugs available to consumers in the United States. The DEA investigates and prosecutes drug gangs and smugglers; collaborates with legislators and policy makers to formulate an effective and comprehensive drug policy; and coordinates with other countries and international organizations to confront international drug smuggling. The DEA is responsible for enforcing prescription drug laws and determining the federal approach to fighting prescription drug abuse. It is in the forefront of prosecuting doctors who run pill mills and participate in smuggling illegal prescription drugs. The DEA publishes *Dateline DEA*, a biweekly electronic newsletter that provides updates on recent campaigns and new policies.

Food and Drug Administration (FDA)
10903 New Hampshire Avenue, Silver Spring, MD 20993
(888) 463-6332
website: www.fda.gov

The Food and Drug Administration (FDA) is an agency of the US Department of Health and Human Services (HHS) tasked with protecting public health through the testing, regulation, and supervision of prescription and over-the-counter medications, contraception, food safety, biopharmaceuticals, medical devices, and more. The FDA is the agency in charge of testing and regulating new drugs on the market through the Center for Drug Evaluation and Research (CDER). The FDA also provides information on drug safety and availability, drug approvals, and the latest science and research. The FDA website features press releases, studies, e-mail alerts, podcasts, and webinars on topics of interest.

Institute of Medicine (IOM)
2100 C Street NW, Washington, DC
(202) 334-2352
e-mail: iomwww@nas.edu
website: www.iom.edu

The Institute of Medicine (IOM) was established in 1970 as the health division of the National Academy of Sciences. The IOM is an independent and nonpartisan organization that "serves as the advisor to the nation to improve health." It does this by conducting extensive research on the nation's emerging health problems and then consults with and advises policy makers and legislators on developing sound public health policy. One of its primary responsibilities is organizing forums, roundtables, conferences, seminars, and other activities that work to facilitate debate, conversation, and the exchange of information. The IOM website offers access to hundreds of in-depth reports and studies published by the organization as well as videos of lectures, speeches, and expert panels.

Narcotics Anonymous (NA)
PO Box 9999, Van Nuys, CA   91409
(818) 773-9999 • fax: (818) 700-0700
e-mail: fsmail@na.org
website: www.na.org

Narcotics Anonymous (NA) is a global, independent, community-based organization that was formed to help individuals recover from drug addiction through a twelve-step program and regular attendance at group meetings, where addicts have access to a support network that will help them attain and maintain a drug-free lifestyle. NA was developed in the 1950s in light of the success of Alcoholics Anonymous (AA), and today NA is a resource for drug addicts all over the world. Local groups organize and run meetings. NA publishes *The NA Way*, a magazine that publishes stories about recovery written by NA members, and *Reaching Out*, a magazine for incarcerated members.

National Institute on Drug Abuse (NIDA)
6001 Executive Boulevard, Room 5213, MSC 9561
Bethesda, MD   20892
(301) 443-1124
e-mail: information@nida.nih.gov
website: www.drugabuse.gov

The National Institute on Drug Abuse (NIDA) is the US institution tasked with conducting scientific research on drug abuse and applying that research to develop programs and strategies to address the problem. One of NIDA's key missions is to improve the efficacy of treatment programs for prescription drug addiction. The NIDA website features educational materials for students and teachers on drugs and drug addiction; a broad range of research reports, including "Prescription Drugs: Abuse and Addiction"; and *NIDA Notes*, a newsletter that updates readers on recent research breakthroughs. Podcasts that include interviews with prominent NIDA scientists discussing recent news and research updates are also available.

Office of National Drug Control Policy (ONDCP)
c/o The White House, 1600 Pennsylvania Avenue NW
Washington, DC   20500
(202) 456-1111
website: www.whitehouse.gov/ondcp

The Office of National Drug Control Policy (ONDCP) develops and coordinates public health strategies to fight drug abuse and address the economic, political, social, and health consequences of drug addiction. Confronting the epidemic of prescription drug abuse is one of ONDCP's top priorities. It also focuses on a "renewed emphasis on community-based prevention programs, early intervention programs in health-care settings, aligning criminal justice policies and public health systems to divert non-violent drug offenders into treatment instead of jail, funding scientific research on drug use, and . . . expanding access to substance abuse treatment." The ONDCP publishes the president's *National Drug Control Strategy*, an annual report on the nation's approach to drug policy. The agency's website features the ONDCP blog, which provides updates on recent initiatives and drug policy.

The Partnership at Drugfree.org
352 Park Avenue South, 9th Floor, New York, NY   10010
(212) 922-1560 • fax: (212) 922-1570
e-mail: webmail@drugfree.org
website: www.drugfree.org

The Partnership at Drugfree.org, formerly known as the Partnership for a Drug-Free America, is a group composed of advertising professionals who strive to reduce teen drug abuse through public service advertising. In recent years, the organization has expanded its work, developing a broad range of online resources for parents searching for help with teen drug addiction. The Partnership at Drugfree.org has also developed community-based education programs on drugs and fighting drug abuse. The organization's website has a Drug Guide that provides information on more than forty commonly abused drugs. The website also features updates on the group's activities and initiatives, access to current research and publications, and a blog that covers topics of interest.

Substance Abuse and Mental Health
Services Administration (SAMHSA)
1 Choke Cherry Road, Rockville, MD   20857
(877) SAMHSA-7 • fax: (240) 221-4292
e-mail: SAMHSAInfo@samhsa.hhs.gov
website: www.samhsa.gov

The Substance Abuse and Mental Health Services Administration (SAMHSA) is an agency of the US Department of Health and Human Services (HHS) that was created to "focus attention, programs, and funding on improving the lives of people with or at risk for mental and substance abuse disorders." SAMHSA publishes statistics on the epidemic of prescription drug abuse and other substances on its website. SAMHSA publications can be found at the National Clearinghouse for Alcohol and Drug Information (NCADI). Many of these works are available via webcast or digital download. The website links to the SAMHSA Substance Abuse Treatment Facility Locator, which helps users find a treatment center near them.

World Health Organization (WHO)
Avenue Appia 20, Geneva 27   1211
 Switzerland
(+41) 22 791 21 11 • fax: (+41) 22 791 31 11
e-mail: info@who.int
website: www.who.int

The World Health Organization (WHO) is the United Nations agency responsible for directing global health care matters. The WHO funds research on health issues that affect global health, including the epidemic of prescription drug abuse. The agency monitors health trends, compiles useful statistics, and offers technical support to countries dealing with the consequences of prescription drug abuse. The WHO website features podcasts, blogs, and videos; it also offers fact sheets, reports, studies, and a calendar of events.

Bibliography of Books

Rod Colvin   *Overcoming Prescription Drug Addiction: A Guide to Coping and Understanding.* 3rd ed. Omaha, NE: Addicus Books, 2008.

Theodore Dalrymple   *Romancing Opiates: Pharmacological Lies and the Addiction Bureaucracy.* New York: Encounter Books, 2006.

James L. Fenley   *Finding a Purpose in the Pain: A Doctor's Approach to Addiction Recovery and Healing.* Las Vegas: Central Recovery Press, 2012.

Rene Fields and Stuart R. Banks, eds.   *Prescription Drug Abuse, Doctor Shopping, and the Role of Medicaid.* Hauppauge, NY: Nova Science Publishers, 2012.

Madelon Lubin Finkel   *Truth, Lies, and Public Health: How We Are Affected When Science and Politics Collide.* Westport, CT: Praeger, 2007.

Erin P. Finley   *Fields of Combat: Understanding PTSD Among Veterans of Iraq and Afghanistan.* Ithaca, NY: ILR Press, 2011.

Gene M. Heyman   *Addiction: A Disorder of Choice.* Cambridge, MA: Harvard University Press, 2009.

Nathan Jacobs and Laura C. Dubois, eds.   *Drug Addiction: Science & Treatment.* Hauppauge, NY: Nova Science Publishers, 2012.

Donald W. Light, ed.   *The Risks of Prescription Drugs.* New York: Columbia University Press, 2010.

Joshua Lyon   *Pill Head: The Secret Life of a Painkiller Addict.* New York: Hyperion, 2009.

Gabor Maté   *In the Realm of Hungry Ghosts: Close Encounters with Addiction.* Berkeley, CA: North Atlantic Books, 2010.

A. Rafik Mohamed and Erik D. Fritsvold   *Dorm Room Dealers: Drugs and the Privileges of Race and Class.* Boulder, CO: Lynne Rienner Publishers, 2010.

Ilana Mountian   *Cultural Ecstasies: Drugs, Gender and the Social Imaginary.* New York: Routledge, 2012.

John J. Philips and Wallace O. Penny, eds.   *Prescription Drugs: Abuse Education and Diversion Control Efforts.* Hauppauge, NY: Nova Science Publishers, 2012.

Richard S. Sandor   *Thinking Simply About Addiction: A Handbook for Recovery.* New York: Jeremy P. Tarcher/Penguin, 2009.

Marvin D. Seppala, with Mark E. Rose   *Prescription Painkillers: History, Pharmacology, and Treatment.* Center City, MN: Hazelden, 2010.

Shlomo Giora Shoham, Moshe Addad, and Martin Kett   *The Insatiable Gorge: An Existentialist View of Opiate Addiction and Its Treatment.* Whitby, Ontario, Canada: De Sitter Publications, 2010.

Michael Stein	*The Addict: One Patient, One Doctor, One Year.* New York: William Morrow, 2009.
Andrea Tone	*The Age of Anxiety: A History of America's Turbulent Affair with Tranquilizers.* New York: Basic Books, 2009.
Andrea Tone and Elizabeth Siegel Watkins, eds.	*Medicating Modern America: Prescription Drugs in History.* New York: New York University Press, 2007.
Ida Walker	*Painkillers: Prescription Dependency.* Philadelphia, PA: Mason Crest Publishers, 2008.

Index

A

Abbott Laboratories, 97, 98
Abt Associates, 159
Abuse-deterrent formulations (ADF), 226
Acceptance therapy, 129–130
Actiq (drug), 158
Acura Pharmaceuticals, 229
Adderall (drug), 70, 73
Addiction
  characteristics of, 202
  to cocaine, 36
  epidemic of, 80–81, 145
  fears, 113, 147–148
  to heroin, 19, 34, 120
  to morphine, 20, 146
  myths, 93
  to opioids, 19, 24, 145, 148
  to OxyContin, 19–20, 78, 98, 114
  physical dependence vs., 91
  problems with, 16–17
  signs of, 73–74
  stigma, 115–116
  to Vicodin, 24–25, 98, 114
  See also Prescription drug abuse; Prescription painkillers
The Age of Anxiety: A History of America's Turbulent Affair with Tranquilizers (Tone), 122–123
Alcohol-Drug Information Center at Indiana University, 73
Alcohol use/abuse
  BAC levels, 45–46
  driving and, 54
  with marijuana, 51
  with opiates, 61
  with oxycodone, 61
Alprazolam (drug), 120, 121, 126
American Academy of Pain Medicine, 88
American Civil Liberties Union (ACLU), 157
American College of Emergency Physicians, 224
American Medical Association, 141, 171, 212, 215
American Pain Foundation, 88
American Pain Society, 198
American Society of Health-System Pharmacists, 71
American Society of Interventional Pain Physicians, 81, 191
Amphetamines (drugs), 48, 71, 73
Annals of Family Medicine (Stange), 172–173, 176
Anti-benzo psychologists, 128
Anti-Drug Abuse Acts, 161
Antidrug coalitions, 225
Associated Press, 157
Ativan (drug), 122
Attention-deficit/hyperactivity disorder (ADHD) drugs
  in colleges and high schools, 73
  increase in, 70–71
  parental abuse of, 71–73
Austria, 137, 166
Aversion technology, 229

B

Balko, Radley, 28–43, 137, 139
Bank of America, 161
Bennett, Tony, 164–165, 166
Bennett, William J., 163–167
Benzodiazepines (drugs)
    benefit of, 121–122, 125
    downside of, 128–129
    drugged driving with, 48, 51
    as miracle cures, 127
    overview, 119–121
    prescription for, 107–108
Bernstein, Ilisa, 182
Black tar heroin epidemic, 188
Blood alcohol concentration
    (BAC), 45–46
Borla, Felicia, 60–61
Boyd, Carol, 98
Bradshaw, Ric, 190
Breggin, Peter, 128
Broward County Sheriff's Office,
    159
Broward County's Medical
    Examiner's Office, 53
Brushwood, David, 37–38
Buprenorphine (drug), 200
BusinessWeek (magazine), 176

C

Cancer treatment
    chronic pain and, 31, 77, 82
    opioids for, 112
    OxyContin for, 19, 145
    prescription painkillers for,
        91–92
Cardiac arrest dangers, 14, 16, 71,
    144
Carey, John, 176

Carnevale Associates, 178–185
Celexa (drug), 121
Center for the Study and Preven-
    tion of Substance Abuse, 53
Centers for Disease Control and
    Prevention (CDC)
    death from prescription
        drugs, 165, 206, 212, 228
    drug overdoses, 24, 80
    drugged driving, 49
    illegal distribution of pre-
        scription drugs, 159
    oxycodone and, 30
    prescription painkiller abuse,
        20, 31–32, 37, 113, 138–139
Centre for Addiction and Mental
    Health, 146
Centres for Pain Management, 147
Chartier, Jeffrey, 120
Cholesterol levels, 30
Chronic headaches, 199
Chronic kidney disease, 29
Chronic pain
    addiction fears, 147–148
    with cancer, 31, 77, 82
    drug controversy over, 146–
        147
    opioid painkillers, 145–146
    overview, 77–78, 80, 144
    prescription drug abuse with,
        79–85, 112–113
    prescription drug monitoring
        programs for, 143–152
    treatment, 30–31, 40, 145,
        149–150
Cialis (drug), 171
Clark, H. Wesley, 121
Clarkin, Sean, 95–105
CNN Money, 159
Cocaine
    addiction to, 36

crack cocaine abuse, 128, 146, 161–162, 188
  deaths from, 36
  drugged driving with, 48
  overdose of, 23, 24
  popularity of, 146
  price of, 159
  teen use of, 99
Coleman, Eric, 191–192
Colombia, 159
Colpe, Lisa, 130
Community Anti-Drug Coalitions of America, 102
Consumer Credit and Protection Act, 148
Consumer Reports (magazine), 168–177
Controlled Substances Act (CSA), 212, 214
Cooley, Steve, 16
Costa, Antonio Maria, 160
Crack cocaine abuse, 128, 146, 161–162, 188

D

Dalhousie University, 145, 152
Davis, Clive, 164
A Day Without Pain (Pohl), 107–108
Decriminalizing drugs
  consumers and marketplace, 157–158
  drug abuse and, 165
  drug policy need, 161–162
  financial sector role, 160–161
  illegal prescription drugs, 158–159
  legalization not successful, 165–167
  overview, 154, 164

prescription drug abuse reduction from, 153–162
  prison-industrial complex, 156–157
  profit from, 160
  rackets over, 154–155
  war on drugs, 155–156, 162
  will not prevent prescription drug abuse, 163
Delta-9-tetrahydrocannabinol (THC), 48
Desperate Housewives (TV show), 71–72
Diazepam (drug), 15
Dingell, John, 175
Direct-to-consumer advertising (DTC)
  drug spending and, 169–170
  fact boxes for, 176–177
  impact of, 174
  legislation for, 171
  opposition to, 171–172
  overview, 169–170
  rebutting industry arguments, 172–173
  regulation of, 168–177
  solution to, 173–175
Disposal of prescription drugs, 27, 63, 218–219
Disposemymeds.org, 27
Dopamine neurotransmitter, 50, 71
Drug Abuse Warning Network (DAWN), 32
Drug Enforcement Administration (DEA)
  doctors as targets by, 37–38, 140
  pain management guidelines by, 38–39
  parents as targets, 70

physician prosecution, 212
physician registration, 214
prescription drug abuse, 31, 32
street gangs, 25
take-back programs, 98, 102, 181
training on prescribed substances, 224
Drug-induced deaths
   CDC reports on, 165, 206, 212, 228
   from cocaine, 36
   of Houston, Whitney, 16, 128, 164, 166, 211, 215
   of Jackson, Michael, 14–16, 120, 164–165, 188
   of Ledger, Heath, 16, 120, 165, 188
   from morphine, 81
   from opioid drugs, 82
   from OxyContin, 32–33, 146, 206
Drug Policy Alliance, 158
Drug wholesalers, 41
Drugged driving
   hazards of, 49–51
   impact of prescription drugs on, 52–58
   overview, 45–46
   with prescription drugs, 44–51
   rates of, 46–48
   statistics on, 56
   by teens, 49
DuPont, Robert, 81

E

ED Advertising Decency Act, 171
Electronic PDMPs
   cost concerns and, 191–192
   guard against abuse, 186–192
   overview, 187
   pill mills and, 187–188
   prescription abuse and, 188–189
   victim need for, 189–190
Ellison, Katherine, 69–74
Engle, Janet, 27
Epperly, Jake, 24
European Monitoring Centre for Drugs and Drug Addiction, 166
Every 15 Minutes program, 60–61

F

Fair Sentencing Act, 161
Federal Communications Commission (FCC), 171
Federal Food, Drug, and Cosmetic Act, 174
The Feminine Mystique (Friedan), 126
Fentanyl (drug), 24, 114
Fibromyalgia, 170, 199
Finland, 166
Fishman, Scott, 88–92, 94
Florida Academy of Pain Medicine, 41
Florida Department of Highway Safety and Motor Vehicles, 57
Florida Medical Examiners Commission, 159
Fort Mill Times (newspaper), 67
Foster, Susan, 206
Freundlich, Naomi, 168–177
Friedan, Betty, 126
Frieden, Thomas, 113
Functional restoration, 92

G

GABA (gamma-aminobutyric acid) neurotransmitter, 50
Garbutt, James, 82
Gateway Foundation, 25
Ghadiali, Murtuza, 197–203
Gharibo, Christopher, 83, 88, 90, 92
GHB (gamma hydroxybutyrate) drug, 50
Global Commission on Drug Policy, 156
Glowacki, Dominick, 120
Goldman, Dana, 207–208
Goldman, Jena, 207–208, 209
Gordon, Barbara, 123
Government-subsidized health care, 34
Greece, 166
Gummy bear drugs, 229–230

H

Hall, Jim, 53
Hamburg, Margaret, 102
Harris, Juan, 66
Harvard University, 124
Hayes, Steven, 125–126, 128
Hazelden Foundation, 89
Health and safety issues, with prescription drugs
    false premise for, 139–141
    overview, 137–138
    priority of, 141–142
    strategy for, 138–139
Health care provider education, 223–225
Health Policy and Clinical Practice, 176

Henderson Police Department, 61, 63
Hentzsch, Cornelia, 148–149
Hernandez, Eleanor, 190
Heroin
    abuse of, 24, 188
    addiction to, 19, 34, 120
    effect on brain, 50
    methadone treatment for addiction, 34
Hillbilly heroin (OxyCondin), 20
Hitti, Miranda, 86–94
HIV/AIDS treatment, 31
Holman, Libby, 229
Houston, Cissy, 166–167
Houston, Whitney, 16, 128, 164, 166, 211, 215
Howard, Ann, 57
Huffington, Arianna, 164, 166
Huffington Post (online news source), 128, 137
Human Rights Watch, 31
Hunter College, 128
Hurwitz, William, 38, 39
Hydrocodone (drug), 24, 61, 113, 141

I

Illegal prescription drugs, 158–159
Illinois Consortium on Drug Policy, 25
I'm Dancing as Fast as I Can (Gordon), 123
Impede Technology, 229
IMS Health, 158
Indiana University, 73
Institute of Medicine, 31, 113
International Drug Evaluation and Classification Programs, 46

Internet (online) pharmacies
  dangers of, 204–209
  drug abuse and, 206
  information on, 206–208
  physician role with, 208–209
  regulation of, 195–196
  role of, 205

J

Jackson, Michael
  conviction of doctor, 211,
    212–214
  drug-induced death of, 14–16,
    120, 164–165, 188
Jameson, Marni, 227–230
Jena, Anupam B., 205
Jones, Bob, 229
Jones, Debra, 80, 84–85
Journal of Analytical Toxicology
  (magazine), 33
Jovey, Roman, 147–148, 150

K

Kane, Ena and Robert, 54–55
Kane, Odette, 54–55
Kane-Willis, Kathleen, 25
Kapoor, Sandeep, 214
Karch, Steven, 35
Katz, Daniel, 23
Katz, Gail and David, 23, 27
Kerlikowske, R. Gil, 102, 136–142
Kessler, Ronald, 124–125
Ketamine drug, 50
Klerman, Gerald, 126
Klonopin (drug), 119, 121, 127,
  130
Krommendyk, Paul, 54

L

Lamm, Brad, 73
Lancet (magazine), 31
Laurie, Fred, 55–57
Ledger, Heath, 16, 120, 165, 188
Legalization of drugs, 165–167
Leonard D. Schaeffer Center for
  Health Policy and Economics,
  207–208
Leonhart, Michele, 102
Libby, Ron, 32–33, 37
Lidocaine (drug), 15
Lipitor (drug), 30, 175–176
Lorazepam (drug), 15
Low-level drug offenders, 156
Lynch, Mary, 144, 146, 152

M

MacCallum, Elizabeth, 143–152
Mail-order pharmacies, 195
Manchikanti, Laxmaiah, 81, 83,
  84, 223
Marijuana (drug)
  alcohol with, 51
  drugged driving and, 47–48,
    49–51, 57
  legal sale of, 158, 166
  popularity of, 61
  reform activists, 32
  teen use of, 99
Maryland Adolescent Survey, 49
Maston, Mary, 29–30, 40–41, 43
Mayday Fund, 78
McCabe, Sean, 98
McGill University, 144
Medical Board of California, 198
Medullary sponge kidney, 29
Mennin, Doug, 128–129

Menstrual cramps, 199
Methadone (drug), 33–35
Methamphetamine (drug), 229
Metropolitan Police Department, 62–63
Midazolam (drug), 15
Miltown (drug), 122–123, 127
Miron, Jeffrey, 156
Moiser, Jeff, 59–63
Monitoring the Future (MTF) survey, 49, 98, 101
Moore, Carol, 150–151
Moran, James P., 171
Morphine (drug)
    addiction to, 20, 146
    death from, 81
    from opioid drugs, 19
    prescription for, 31, 92
    side effects from, 149
Morrisette, Sunny, 72–73
Morton, Dale, 230
Mothers Against Drunk Driving, 45
Murphy, Brittany, 165
Murray, Conrad, 14–16, 212–214

N

Nadelmann, Ethan, 158
Nadler, Jerrold, 171
Narcotics Overdose Prevention and Education (NOPE), 191
National Association of Attorneys General, 39
National Association of Boards of Pharmacy (NABP), 195–196
National Center on Addiction and Substance Abuse, 206
National Drug Control Strategy, 138–140, 179

National Highway Traffic Safety Administration (NHTSA), 46, 54, 57
National Institute on Drug Abuse (NIDA)
    Aderall abuse, 73
    drugged driving and, 44–51
    drugs that can't be abused, 228
    parental drug abuse, 70–71
    prescription drug addictions, 83, 88, 102
    prescription drug crisis, 31
National Institutes of Health, 124
National Pain Summit, 141
National Prescription Drug Take-Back Days, 182
National Roadside Survey, 46
National Rx Drug Abuse Summit, 228
National Security Decision Directive, 155
National Survey on Drug Use and Health (NSDUH), 36, 47, 97, 101, 180
National Youth Anti-Drug Media Campaign, 100–103
Nauuert, Rick, 204–209
Nerve-damaged patients, 150
Neuroscience Education Institute, 120
New Hope Recovery Center, 24, 27
Nielsen Media Research, 169–170
Nixon, Richard, 155, 160, 162
Nociceptive pain, 77
Nonrheumatoid arthritis, 199
Nonviolent drug crimes, 162
Not in My House (website), 97, 103

Nova Southeastern University, 53
Novellino, Teresa, 157–158
NYU Hospital for Joint Diseases, 88
NYU Langone Medical Center, 88

O

Obama, Barack (administration), 137–138, 161, 179
Occupy Wall Street movement, 154
Odom, Stephen, 72
Office of Controlled Substances, 149
Office of Drug Control, 134
Office of National Drug Control Policy (ONDCP), 102–103, 165, 179, 220–226
Online pharmacies. *See* Internet (online) pharmacies
Opioid drugs
    addiction to, 19, 24, 145, 148
    for chronic pain, 145–146
    death from, 82
    drugged driving with, 48
    levels in body of, 35
    need for, 150–152
    overdose from, 81
    treatment plans including, 90, 115
Opioid Risk Evaluation and Mitigation Strategy (REMS), 224, 225
Over-the-counter drugs (OTC). *See* Prescription drug abuse
Owens, Dee, 73, 74
Oxecta (drug), 229
Oxycodone (drug)
    abuse of, 148
    addiction to, 19

    with alcohol, 61
    buying from pill mills, 187–188
    deterrents to abuse of, 228
    drugged driving with, 55
    illegal distribution of, 159
    regulation of, 30
OxyContin (drug)
    abuse of, 101
    addiction to, 19–20, 78, 98, 114
    in Canada, 149
    for cancer treatment, 19, 145
    death from, 32–33, 146, 206
    as delisted, 145
    demand for, 198–199
    effect on brain, 50
    as hillbilly heroin, 20
    illegal distribution of, 158, 159, 188
    online purchase of, 205
    overdose on, 23, 148–149
    pharm parties and, 65–66
    prescription of, 34, 148
    usage trends, 62
OxyNeo (drug), 145, 149

P

Pain management guidelines by DEA, 38–39
Pain Medicine (magazine), 139–140
Pakistan, 159
Parental abuse of childrens' drugs, 69–74
Parental education, 225
Parents. The Anti-Drug (website), 216–219
Park Slope Food Coop, 127

Partnership at Drugfree.org, 96, 105

Partnership Attitude Tracking Study (PATS), 97, 100

Partnership for a Drug-Free America, 166

Patient education, 225

Patient screening improvements
  demand for painkillers, 198–199
  overview, 198
  physician challenges with, 199–200
  practitioner help with, 200
  prevent abuse, 197–203
  SOAPP-5 treatment, 202–203
  step-by-step approach, 201–202

Pating, David, 197–203

Paul, Keith, 61–62

Paulozzi, Leonard, 80–82

PCP (phencyclidine) drug, 50

Percocet (drug), 32, 78, 114, 159, 188, 229

Perry, Karen, 190–191

Perry, Rich, 190

Pharm (phishing) parties
  assessment of problem, 61–62
  existence of, 67–68
  as myth, 64–68
  overview, 65
  risk from, 60
  threat to teens, 59–63

Pharmaceutical companies/industry
  addiction help from, 103
  blame for drug abuse, 198–199
  drug abuse blame, 111–117
  drug abuse research, 158
  drug use deterrents, 228
  health reform and, 169
  not to blame for drug abuse, 111–117
  physician over prescription of drugs, 106–110
  See also Direct-to-consumer advertising

Pharmaceutical Research and Manufacturers of America (PhRMA), 169, 172

Pharmacies
  break-ins, 145, 146
  painkiller supplies from, 41–42, 133, 141, 188
  subpoena for records, 215
  training from, 222, 224–225
  See also Internet (online) pharmacies

Pharmacoepidemiology and Drug Safety (Paulozzi), 81

Pharmacological Calvinism, 129

Pilkington, Ed, 186–192

Pill mills, 42, 98, 187–188

Pohl, Mel, 107–108

Polydrug use, 55

Portfolio.com, 157

Portugal, 166

Prescription drug abuse
  addiction vs. physical dependence, 91
  addressing problem of, 62–63
  brain impact and, 50
  cardiac arrest dangers, 14, 16, 71, 144
  chronic pain, 77–78
  doctor shopping, 83
  as epidemic, 80–81, 206
  functional restoration, 92
  increase in addicts, 81–83
  as major problem, 19–21, 180
  myths over, 86–94

overview, 14–17, 87
polydrug use, 55
ready access to, 95–105
threat of, 61
trends in, 62
See also Drugged driving;
Teen prescription drug abuse
Prescription drug abuse, prevention
dangers of online pharmacies, 204–209
education as key to, 220–226
with new technology, 227–230
overview, 195–196
patient screening improvements, 197–203
prosecution of doctors, 210–215
Prescription Drug Abuse Prevention Plan, 179
Prescription Drug Marketing Act (1987), 169
Prescription drug monitoring programs (PDMPs)
balance of health and safety, 136–142
chronic pain and, 143–152
decriminalizing drugs, 153–162
defined, 189
opioid abuse and, 183
overview, 133–135
regulating advertising, 168–177
See also Decriminalizing drugs; Electronic PDMPs
Prescription painkillers
abuse and undertreatment, 37–38
abuse contributors, 25–26
addressing problem of, 42–43
campaign against, 25–26

case for a crisis, 31–32
CDC reports on, 20, 31–32, 37, 113, 138–139
challenging overdose statistics, 32–33
debate over epidemic, 28–43
demand for, 39–40, 198–199
disposal of, 27, 63, 218–219
epidemic of, 22–27
methadone, 33–35
misunderstandings about, 24–25
new laws for, 40–42
overdoses from, 23–24
overview, 23, 29–30
questionable diagnoses, 35–37
safe disposal of, 27
safe treatment with, 38–39
from unscrupulous doctors, 16, 37, 42
See also Health and safety issues
Prescription painkillers, physician over prescription
addiction fears, 113
addiction stigma, 115–116
of benzodiazepines, 119–122
by-product of modern life, 118–130
chronic pain treatment, 112–113
drug abuse blame, 111–117
integrative medicine, 108
of Miltown, 122–123
overview, 107, 112
personal responsibility and, 116–117
pharmaceutical companies and, 106–110
truth about, 114–115
Prison-industrial complex, 156–157

Propofol (drug), 15, 212–213
Prostate cancer pain, 92
Prozac (drug), 121, 124
Psychiatry (magazine), 124
Psychotropic drugs, 48
Purdue Pharma, 19–20, 103, 199, 228
Purdue Pharma Canada, 148–149

Q

Qing Dynasty, 144
Queen Elizabeth II Health Sciences Centre, 145

R

Ratner, Ellen, 106–110
Ray, Albert, 41, 42
Ready access to prescription drugs, 95–105
Reagan, Nancy, 155, 157
Reagan, Ronald, 155
Recreational painkillers. *See* Prescription painkillers
Rheumatoid arthritis pain, 80
Ritalin (drug), 50, 72, 205
Roberts, Ellen, 54, 57–58
Rohypnol (drug), 50
Roosevelt University's Illinois Consortium on Drug Policy, 25
Rosen, David, 152–162
Roxicodone (drug), 188
Ryan Haight Online Pharmacy Consumer Protection Act, 208

S

Safe and Drug-Free Schools and Communities state grant program, 101

Say No to Drug Ads, 171
Schueler, Harold, 53, 55
Schumer, Charles, 113
Scott, Rick, 30, 134–135, 191
Seattle Times (newspaper), 34
Selby, Peter, 146
Selective serotonin reuptake inhibitors (SSRIs), 121, 124
Seppala, Marvin, 89, 93
Shafer, Jack, 64–68
Simeone Associates Inc., 183
Situational anxiety, 124–126
Sloman, Jeffrey, 161
Smith, Anna Nicole, 16, 165, 188, 214
Smith, Krista, 84
SOAPP-5 (Screener and Opiate Assessment for People with Pain), 202–203
Somerville, Margaret, 144
Stahl, Stephen, 120
Stange, Kurt C., 172–173
Stimulants (drugs)
  abuse of, 70, 73, 99
  addiction to, 15
  defined, 72
  drugged driving with, 48, 56
  prescriptions for, 71
  Ritalin, 50, 72, 205
Stracar, Angela, 54–55
Street gangs, 25
Streeter, Angel, 52–58
Stupak, Bart, 175
Substance Abuse and Mental Health Services Administration (SAMHSA), 24, 120–121, 158, 180
Substance abuse training, 222–223
Szabo, Liz, 79–85
Szalavitz, Maia, 111–117

T

Take-back programs
    assessment of, 183–184
    event-based vs. ongoing, 181
    FDA guidelines, 182
    limit access to medications,
        178–185
    overview, 179–181
    recommendations for, 184
    as solution, 185
    support for, 98, 102
Tauzin, Billy, 172
Tea Party, 191
Teen prescription drug abuse
    access concerns, 97–98
    awareness campaigns, 102–103
    contributing factors to, 97–
        102
    drugged driving, 49
    motivations of, 97–98
    moving forward, 104–105
    overview, 96–97
    parental role in, 99–100, 216–
        219
    prevalence of, 218
    prevention efforts against,
        100–102
    ready access to, 95–105
    risk perception by, 98
    stakeholders against, 103–104
    trends in, 101
Thayer, Tyson, 62
Thomas, Monifa, 22–27
Thoren, Sally, 24–25
Time (magazine), 38, 66, 67, 175
Tone, Andrea, 122–123
Trachtman, Erica, 210–215
Treatment Research Institute, 102

U

United Nations Commission on
    Narcotic Drugs, 137
United Nations drug conventions,
    31
United Nations Office on Drugs
    and Crime, 160
United Nations Universal Declara-
    tion of Human Rights, 145
University of California, Davis
    School of Medicine, 88
University of Florida College of
    Pharmacy, 37
University of Illinois, 27
University of Michigan, 98, 99
University of Nevada, 125
University of North Carolina Hos-
    pitals, 81
University of Southern California,
    208
Unscrupulous doctors, 16, 37, 42
US Department of Health and
    Human Services, 110, 158
US Food and Drug Administra-
    tion (FDA)
    direct-to-consumer advertis-
        ing, 174
    drug approval by, 19
    experimental painkillers, 113
    Internet pharmacies and, 208
    OxyContin promotion and,
        148
    pharmaceutical industry over-
        sight, 172–173
    public education against
        abuse, 102

V

Valium (drug), 33, 119, 123

Verified Internet Pharmacy Practice Sites (VIPPS) program, 195–196

Veterans Administration, 198

Vicodin (drug)
    abuse of, 101
    addiction to, 24–25, 98, 114
    banning ads for, 171
    for chronic pain, 84
    cost of, 159
    deterrent to abuse of, 229

Village Voice (newspaper), 38

Volkow, Nora, 83, 84, 102, 228

W

Wachovia Bank, 161

Waldock, Katherine, 156

Wall Street Journal (newspaper), 38

War on drugs, 155–156, 162

Waxman, Henry, 171, 175

Weill Cornell Medical College, 129

Weiss, Susan, 88–90, 89–90

Wells Fargo bank, 161

Winehouse, Amy, 164

Winfrey, Oprah, 166–167

Woloshin, Steven, 177

X

Xanax (drug)
    defined, 119–121
    drugged driving with, 53–55
    Houston, Whitney, use of, 211
    illegal distribution of, 158
    as miracle cure, 127
    online purchase of, 205
    overuse of, 128, 130
    overview, 123–124, 126

Z

Zegeye, Beruch, 54

Zoloft (drug), 57, 120

Zvara, David, 81, 82, 84

CPSIA information can be obtained
at www.ICGtesting.com
Printed in the USA
FFOW02n1739140614
5907FF